Nolan Ryan

The Road to Cooperstown

By Nolan Ryan

with T.R. Sullivan

and Mickey Herskowitz

Houston Chronicle

HOUSTON'S LEADING INFORMATION SOURCE

www.houstonchronicle.com

Fort Worth Star-Telegram

Howard, Ryan and Godwin Make All-District

NOLAN RYAN

stricks out 17 Tigers

...n record wi.. row 1... ...tory over La Marque, here on Friday night. Again the major factor in the win was pitcher Nolan Ryan, who struck out seventeen La Marque batters while allowing only tw... hits. Ryan's strikeout... through four district ga... is 59.

The Yell...

...day nigh...
. Benefield was chosen the Most Outstanding Player in the tournament. David King and Nolen Ryan of Alvin were selected to the all-tourney team along with Butch Brew... er, Angleton; Ray C... Hitchcock; and Monte Un...

NOLEN RYAN

RUTH HOLDORFF
Girls District Tennis

conly

ALVIN, TEXAS 1964

NEW YORK METS PROSPECT CARD

ELIGIBLE TO SIGN 1965 —

RYAN, Lynn Nolan RHP
LAST NAME   FIRST NAME   MIDDLE NAME   POS.   PROSPECT RATING

ADDRESS 719 DEZZO ALVIN, TEXAS
        STREET   CITY   STATE

TELEPHONE 713-585-2627

HT 6'-½ WGT 145 B R T R RACE W MARRIED

DATE OF BIRTH 1-31-47   AGE 17

TEAM ALVIN HIGH SCHOOL — ALVIN, TEXAS
COLL. J.C. H.S. LEGION AMATEUR CITY STATE

GRADUATION DATE MAY — 1965

	PITCHER				
FB	CB	CON	CH	SL	KN
8	10	2	2	—	—

NO. OF GAMES 4-25-64 1

INNINGS PITCHED 1   1

HAS NOT REGISTERED —

SCOUT FIELD NOTES This SKINNY HIGH SCHOOL JUNIOR HAS THE
BEST ARM I HAVE EVER SEEN IN MY LIFE. This KID
RYAN THROWS MUCH HARDER THAN Jim MALONEY OF
THE CINCINATTI REDS, OR TURK FARREL OF THE HOUSTON
COLT .45s (I SAW THEM PITCH THURSDAY NITE 4-23-64.)
RYAN HAS THE POTENTIAL TO BE A HIGH PERFORMANCE
STARTING PITCHER ON A MAJOR LEAGUE STAFF.
A SMILING FRIENDLY FACED KID-WIDE SHOULDERS LONG
ARMS & STRONG HANDS.   SCOUT Red Murff   DATE 4-26-64
    GOOD ATHLETE.   TIME GRADED 12:00 (HIGH NOON) 4-25-64

Published by Addax Publishing Group, Inc.
Copyright © 1999 by Nolan Ryan

For Information address:
Addax Publishing Group, Inc.
8643 Hauser Drive, Suite 235, Lenexa, KS 66215

Bob Snodgrass
Publisher

Jerry Hirt
Art Direction/Design

An Beard
Managing Editor

Darcie Kidson
Publicity

Development assistance: Michelle Zwickle-Washington, Sharon Snodgrass, Nelson Elliott
Mike Bynum, Lois Heathman

ISBN: 1-886110-82-4

Printed in the USA

1 3 5 7 9 10 8 6 4 2

ATTENTION: SCHOOLS AND BUSINESSES
Addax Publishing Group, Inc. books are available at quantity discounts with bulk purchase for education, business, or sales promotional use. For information, please write to: Special Sales Department, Addax Publishing Group, 8643 Hauser Drive, Suite 235, Lenexa, Kansas 66215

Library of Congress Catalog Number: 99-75483

Truly the
RINGMASTER

1969
World Champion
New York Mets

1972
American League
All-Star

1973
American League
All-Star

1975
American League
All-Star

1979
American League
All-Star

1981
National League
All-Star

1985
National League
All-Star

1989
American League
All-Star

1995

Displayed at Nolan Ryan Center, Alvin, Texas

To my parents,

who taught me to be responsible

and hard-working.

Also to my wonderful family,

Ruth, Reid, Reese and Wendy,

without whom, I would not be where I am today.

And to all of my former teammates,

I take a piece of

each of you to the Hall of Fame.

-Nolan Ryan

1968 METS' ROOKIE STARS

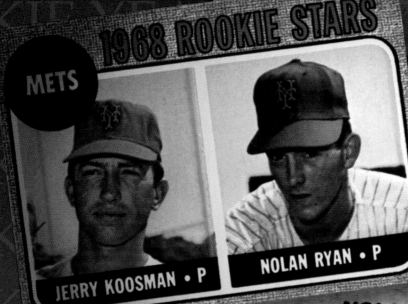

1968 ROOKIE STARS

METS

JERRY KOOSMAN • P

NOLAN RYAN • P

KOOSMAN—PITCHER

4, Jerry made a big splash
in 1966 when he won 12
npiled a 1.38 E.R.A. for Au-
thpaw won 11 games at
t year.

IFETIME PITCHING RECORD

	PCT.	SO	BB	ERA
3		496	156	2.60

NOLAN RYAN—PITCHER

In 1966, Nolan had a senational 17-2 record with Greenville. That year he struck
out 313 batters! The 21 year old righthander is one of the most promising
rookies in the majors.

MINOR LEAGUE LIFETIME PITCHING RECORD

W	L	PCT.	SO	BB	ERA
21	10	.677	445	200	2.81

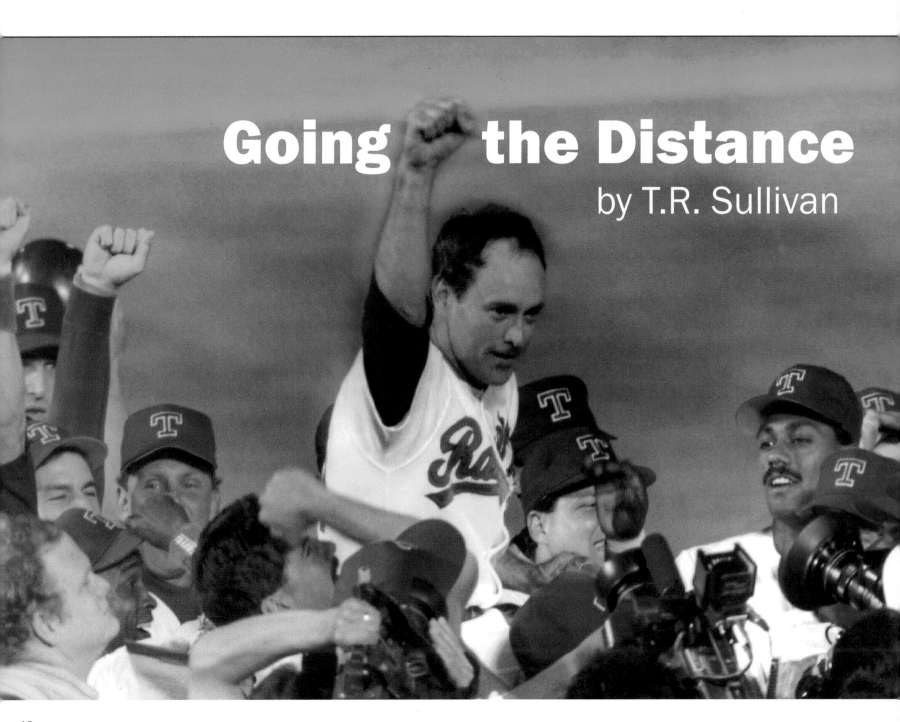

Going the Distance

by T.R. Sullivan

Nolan Ryan woke up on Jan. 5, 1999, feeling nervous and edgy. Normally such feelings were reserved for big games, like the day he drove to Arlington Stadium in anticipation of getting his 5,000th strikeout and missed the turnoff.

But that was 10 years before. And it had been more than five years since Ryan had pitched in a major league game.

Still, there was something else on his mind that January morning at his 80-acre spread in the southeast Texas town of Alvin.

"He was a lot more nervous and quiet," his wife Ruth said. "I knew he was in a reflective mood."

Ryan was waiting for a phone call. It was supposed to come shortly

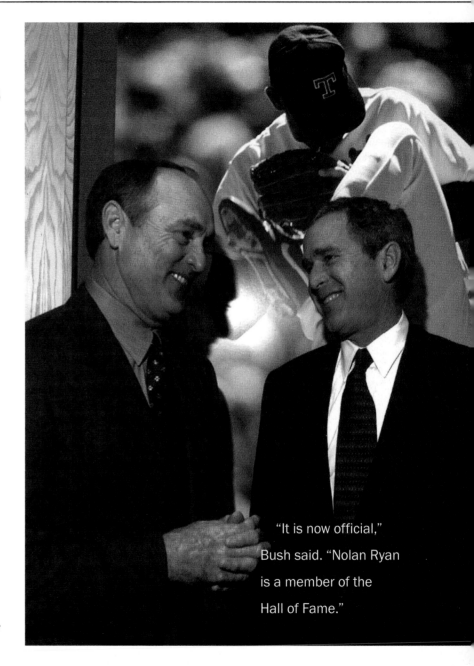

"It is now official," Bush said. "Nolan Ryan is a member of the Hall of Fame."

after noon and he tried to occupy his mind by writing Christmas thank-you notes.

"I can honestly say I didn't give it a whole lot of thought until I woke up and thought, 'What if I don't get that call," Ryan said. "There was a little bit of apprehension. You really don't know how people view you or how they'll vote. It's just one of those things."

His son Reese was busy preparing deer backstrap fajitas for lunch when the phone call finally came. He heard what he wanted to hear.

A few hours later, a couple hundred people jammed a small auditorium at the Nolan Ryan Center at Alvin Community College.

There were reporters and television crews present from all over the state. Ruth was there with the Ryans' three children, sons Reid and Reese and daughter Wendy. The rest of the audience was made up of friends and neighbors from Alvin, a town Ryan has called home for almost all of his 52 years.

They watched expectantly as George W. Bush, governor of the state of Texas, walked to the podium and made the announcement.

"It is now official," Bush said. "Nolan Ryan is a member of the Hall of Fame."

The auditorium burst into applause and Bush went on to tell them Ryan had received 491 of 497 possible votes from the Baseball Writers Association of America – six short of being the first player elected unanimously. The 98.79 percent approval was second in history, trailing only the 98.84 percent received by Ryan's friend and ex-teammate Tom Seaver.

"We're going to be looking for those six writers who must have never seen him play," Bush said.

It would be difficult to find any baseball fan in America who never saw Ryan play, either in person or on television. He pitched in 807 games and 5,386 innings in a career that spanned a major league record 27 seasons.

He pitched for the New York Mets, California Angels, Houston Astros and the Texas Rangers. The Mets were the only ones not to retire his number. He started during the height of the Vietnam War and was still going strong during the Gulf War.

He won 324 games, pitched seven no-hitters and struck out an astounding 5,714 batters. In the process he became one of the most legendary players to ever wear a baseball uniform.

Only John Wayne could play the part in a movie. Tall, strong and

Ryan won 324 games, pitched seven no-hitters and struck out an astounding 5,714 batters.

proud, Ryan was born, raised and lives the life of a Texan, at home on one of his three cattle ranches as much as a pitching mound.

He was admired for his personal integrity as much as he was for the 100 mile-per-hour fastball that was known as the Ryan Express.

Bush, once a part-owner of the Rangers, said, "(Someone) once said that to know the hearts and minds of Americans, you'd better know baseball. Well, to know the hearts and minds of Texans, you'd better know Nolan Ryan. He's as Texas as a Texan can be.

"He's very typical of what you can expect from a frontier Texan. There is a brilliance in his simplicity and it accentuates why Texans see him as a hero. The one thing you can say about him as a true hero is that he has never failed us."

He has co-authored four books: two autobiographies and two books about pitching. He has made commercials for airlines, boots and blue jeans, pain-reliever medicine and office equipment. He owns three cattle ranches, two banks, an inn, a restaurant and a minor

Ryan acknowledges the chanting crowd after his 300th win against the Brewers.

league baseball team. He serves as a commissioner for the Texas Parks and Wildlife Department.

At one point, his rookie baseball card was valued at $1,000. Fans once lined up around the block at an Anaheim, Calif. hotel in the hopes of getting his autograph. One fan even interrupted Ryan eating dinner at a restaurant and asked him to autograph the cast covering his broken foot.

During spring training, the Rangers had a sign posted outside their private parking lot which read: "Nolan Ryan signing autographs today." When fans saw that sign posted they would line up by the hundreds. The problem was that people kept stealing the sign.

They admired their hero as much as the sportswriter who asked for and received the sanitary socks Ryan wore the night he won his 300th game in Milwaukee. The red clay has yet to be washed out.

"He's like Joe DiMaggio," former Houston general manager Al Rosen said. "You respond to him. There's a sense of majesty."

Said his former California Angels manager Dick Williams, "I would like my son to be like him."

That would be difficult. Nolan Ryan was one of a kind.

"He's very typical of what you can expect from a frontier Texan. There is a brilliance in his simplicity and it accentuates why Texans see him as a hero. The one thing you can say about him as a true hero is that he has never failed us."

-George W. Bush, governor of the state of Texas

Nolan Ryan once called Alvin "my natural and spiritual home."

Long after he became a pitching legend making millions of dollars, Ryan and his family were still making their home in Alvin, a farm and ranching community of 19,000 people located 30 miles south of Houston.

Ryan was born in Refugio, Tex., but his family moved to Alvin when he was six weeks old. It's been his home ever since. He lives on a ranch east of town rather than the four-bedroom house on Dezso Drive where he grew up, but Ryan has never seriously considered making his home anywhere else.

He married his high school sweetheart and his three children, Reid,

Reese and Wendy, all graduated from Alvin High School. Ryan remains an important member of the community as Chairman of the Board of The Express Bank of Alvin and overseer of the Nolan Ryan Center at Alvin Community College.

"Ruth and I had a great childhood in Alvin," Ryan said. "It was a great place to grow up so we wanted to give our children the same experience. Early on in my career we basically decided that no matter where I was playing, Alvin would always be our home."

Ryan was born January 31, 1947, the youngest of six children of Lynn Nolan and Martha Lee Ryan. His father worked for an oil company and his mother chose Alvin as the place they would live because of the good schools and the live oak trees that grace the town's streets.

When Ryan was still going strong in his mid-40s, he would often look back and give his parents credit for his much-admired work ethic.

Ryan's father was a supervisor at a local refinery but when his children started nearing college age, he took a second job as the local distributor for *The Houston Post*. For many years, Ryan, his father and his brother, Robert, would get up at one in the morning and deliver newspapers. When they were finished, it was time for Nolan to go to school and his father to go to work.

The rest of the time he spent playing sports, baseball and basketball in particular. The first no-hitter came as a Little Leaguer and he was an All-Star at the ages of 11 and 12.

"I knew I had an exceptional arm, but that was as far as my ability went," Ryan said.

One year, after his Little League All-Star team had been eliminated from the post-season tournament, a man giving a speech in the closing ceremonies said,

"One day, one of you Little Leaguers will go on to play in the major leagues."

Ryan went home and told his mom, "That man was talking about me."

Ryan's favorite sport in high school was basketball. He played center because he was 6-foot-2 and his team went 27-4 two years in a row. For a time he seriously considered going to junior college on a basketball

scholarship. His sweetheart and later wife, Ruth, teamed with Rachel Adams to win the Class 3A state doubles tennis title and was "All School Most Beautiful" three years running.

Ryan was the star of the baseball team as well. He threw incredibly hard but had no idea where the ball was going.

"There were problems with catchers who were afraid to catch him or couldn't hold onto the ball, it moved so much," his high school coach, Jim Watson, said. "Nolan didn't exactly know where the ball was going, but he didn't exactly have to thread a needle back then. Those kids were so scared, they'd swing at anything just to get out of there. He'd average 15, 16 strikeouts sometimes in those seven-inning games."

New York Mets scout Red Murff stumbled onto Ryan during his sophomore year. He was on his way to scout a game in Galveston when he stopped by a tournament in Alvin.

"I've never seen an arm like that in my life." *-Red Murff*

Ryan had just come in to pitch and threw two fastballs that left Murff thunderstruck. He had never seen a high school pitcher throw that hard. Later that night he saw Jim Maloney of the Cincinnati Reds pitch against Houston's Turk Farrell and realized those two pitchers, who both threw around 95 miles per hour, couldn't throw as hard as the skinny kid he had seen that afternoon in Alvin.

Murff was amazed that Ryan was just a sophomore, telling his coach, Jim Watson, "I've never seen an arm like that in my life."

Murff would spend the next three years watching that arm carefully. He even told Watson not to call in Ryan's performances to the Houston papers, insisting the publicity would affect his concentration. Murff was really afraid other scouts would catch on to Ryan. They never did. Those who watched him pitch were turned off by his lack of control.

The Mets selected Ryan in the eighth round of the 1965 draft. There were 294 players taken ahead of him. Ryan was still undecided whether to get a job, go to college or play baseball. Finally, Murff

offered Ryan a $30,000 bonus.

They were sitting around the kitchen table with his parents and a local sportswriter. Ryan hesitated, then looked at his father and realized how hard he would have to work to get that kind of money.

Ryan signed the contract and went off to play professional baseball.

The New York Mets were not a good baseball team. They lost a major league record 120 games in 1962, their first year as an expansion team, and the only real entertainment was their manager Casey Stengel. Their best players — Duke Snider, Gil Hodges, Richie Ashburn and Warren Spahn — were all way past their prime.

But while they were stumbling and bumbling at the major league level, they were quietly putting together some outstanding young talent in the minors. The pitching was especially good. Ryan was one. There was also Tom Seaver, an All-American from USC, Jerry Koosman, Tug McGraw and Gary Gentry.

Ryan started out at Marion, Va., in the Appalachian League, going 3-6 with a 4.38 ERA. But he also struck out 115 in 78 innings.

He was a sensation the following year in Greenville, S.C., in the Class A Western Carolina League. It was there Ryan first started drawing comparisons to Sandy Koufax and created the kind of excitement that would follow him around the rest of his career.

He was 17-2 with a 2.51 ERA and led the league with 272 strikeouts. In one seven-inning game, he struck out 19 batters. On another occasion, he struck out 21 in 10 innings. He was exciting even to watch warm up. Once a pitch got away and hit a woman who was leaning against the backstop. She suffered a broken arm.

The Mets brought him up at the end of the year. His major league debut was Sept. 11, 1966, against the Atlanta Braves. Joe Torre hit a home run off him while pitcher Pat Jarvis was the first of 5,714 strikeouts.

"I don't remember it at all," Ryan said. "The thing I remember about that game was I was 19 and very nervous. The Braves had all those great hitters who, four or five years before, were in my baseball card collection."

The New York years of 1966-71 were

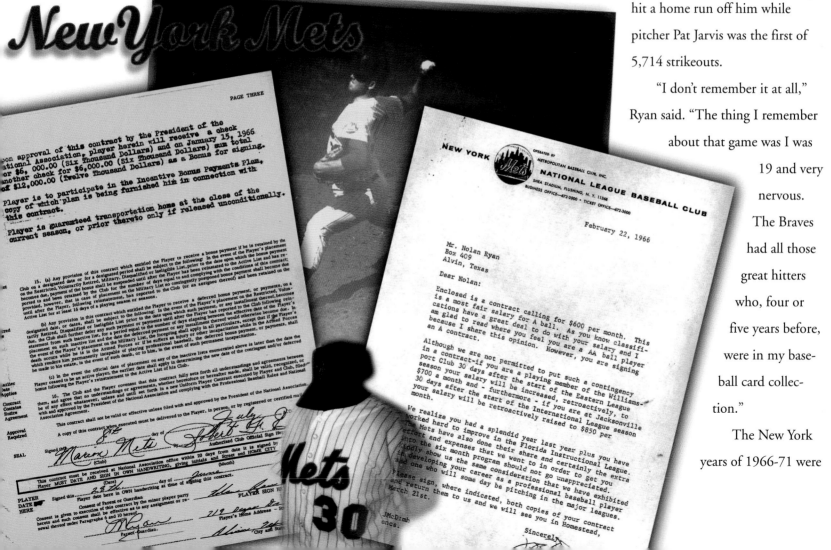

mostly frustrating ones for Ryan. He was rushed to the majors even though he still didn't know how to pitch. He was also held back because of arm injuries and — at the height of the Vietnam War — Army Reserve duty. He also suffered from frequent blisters. All that kept him from pitching regularly.

He won the third and clinching game of the League Championship Series with seven strong innings in relief and he got a save in Game three of the World Series by throwing 2⅔ scoreless innings in the Mets' 5-0 victory over the Baltimore Orioles.

After missing 1967 with arm injuries, Ryan won his first major league game on April 14, 1968, with a 4-0 victory against the Houston Astros. He pitched 6 2/3 scoreless innings.

The Mets finished 73-89 in 1968 and in ninth place. They were 100-1 favorites to win the World Series in 1969 – the first season in which the leagues were split into two divisions.

But the Miracle Mets, as they were called that year, shocked the country by overcoming the Chicago Cubs in September to win the division title. Ryan, still pitching irregularly because of Army duty, was 6-3 with a 3.54 ERA in 25 games, including 10 starts.

His most important game was a 7-1 complete game victory over the Montreal Expos on Sept. 10, which gave the Mets a one-game lead over the Cubs.

He did not start a game in post-season but had two important relief appearances. He won the third and clinching game of the League Championship Series with seven strong innings in relief and he got a save in Game Three of the World Series by throwing 2⅔ scoreless innings in the Mets' 5-0 victory over the Baltimore Orioles.

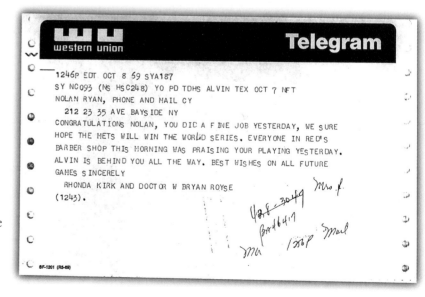

When the Mets finally wrapped up the series, Ryan said, "I knew I had contributed to the team's success. The World Series had helped restore some of my confidence in my ability and my desire to play. Yet I still felt like a guy on the outside looking in. My role on the Mets was unclear."

Nolan and Ruth, two native Texans, were also very uncomfortable living in the nation's largest city.

"I felt like McCloud, the cop on TV who's forced to work in New York," Ryan said. "I just felt totally lost there."

Ryan would stay two more years, going 7-11 with a 3.41 ERA in 1970 and 10-14 with a 3.97 ERA in 1971. He was still the hardest thrower on the Mets talented staff but quite unpolished, especially when compared to Tom Seaver and Jerry Koosman.

Finally Ryan suggested to general manager Bob Scheffing that he should be traded. The Mets were willing to accommodate him. They had enough pitching.

What they really needed was a third baseman.

Organized baseball has been around for over 125 years. The National League came into existence in 1876. It is often difficult to make comparisons between eras on intangible questions such as who was the best player or what was the best World Series.

But many people believe one of the most lopsided trades ever made in baseball history was completed on Dec. 10, 1971, when the Mets traded Nolan Ryan along with pitcher Don Rose, catcher Francisco Estrada and outfielder Leroy Stanton to the California Angels for shortstop Jim Fregosi.

The deal originally looked good for the Mets. Fregosi was 29, a six-time All-Star and a prime candidate to end the Mets' perennial problems at third base. The players they gave up were all young and unproven.

Ryan quickly changed that, once he met Angels pitching coach Tom Morgan.

His fastball also had a nickname, the Ryan Express. His reputation grew with each game.

"Of all the pitching coaches I've had, Tom Morgan probably had the biggest influence on my career," Ryan said. "Morgan was the one who really worked with me on my mechanics, smoothed out my delivery and really helped me gain control of my pitches."

Morgan also convinced Angels manager Del Rice to keep Ryan in the rotation when he was struggling early in the 1972 season. The patience paid off as Ryan had a breakthrough year, going 19-16 with a 2.28 ERA. He also was selected for the American League All-Star team and led the league with 329 strikeouts.

His fastball also had a nickname, the Ryan Express. His reputation grew with each game.

"He's spectacular," said Cleveland broadcaster Herb Score, once a great pitcher himself. "With someone like Ryan there is always the possibility of a strikeout record or a no-hitter."

"You don't face Ryan without your rest," Reggie Jackson said. "He's the only guy I go against that makes me go to bed before midnight."

"He's spectacular," said Cleveland broadcaster Herb Score, once a great pitcher himself. "With someone like Ryan there is always the possibility of a strikeout record or a no-hitter."

Every great player has at least one season that defines his career. Ryan had two of them and the first came in 1973.

The Angels were 79-83 and finished fourth. There's no telling where they would have finished without Ryan. There's also no telling

Ryan's major-league record of 383 strikeouts against Boston broke the American League record held by Bob Feller.

what his record would have been had he pitched with a decent ballclub.

What is known is that Ryan struck out 383 batters, breaking the all-time single-season record of 382, set by Sandy Koufax in 1965. He also started on the road to another immortal record.

Ryan, getting ready to pitch against the Kansas City Royals, said that on May 15, 1973, "A no-hitter was the farthest thing from my mind. I remember warming up and feeling bad in the bullpen. I had poor mechanics and I couldn't get the curve ball over, and I was feeling pretty frustrated.

"I remember walking out of the bullpen and telling the guys in the bullpen, somebody better get ready. I don't think I'm going to be out there too long. The first couple of innings went along the lines of how it was going in the bullpen.

"But I got through them, and things started getting better. I got better as the game went on, as was my pattern back in those days."

READY FOR CELEBRATION — Angel pitcher Nolan Ryan accepts congratulations from fellow pitcher Bill Singer (48) after walking off the mound following Sunday's no-hitter against Detroit. It was Ryan's second "perfecto" of the season. He struck out 17 Tigers, miss- ing the American League record of 18. Ryan is the pitcher in 20 years to throw two no-hit games in some season. The 41,411 Detro[it] [fans] gave R[yan] standing ovation when the game finished. (UPI Tel[e])

Ryan ended up walking three and striking out 12. But he did not allow a hit, the first no-hitter of his career.

Two months later, Ryan had a much better feeling about his warmups in the bullpen before getting ready to pitch against the Detroit Tigers.

Ryan told Morgan, "If I ever pitch a no-hitter, it will be today."

He did, with possibly the most dominating performance of his career. He walked four and struck out 17. One of those strikeouts was Norm Cash in the second inning.

As Cash walked back to the bench, teammate Bill Freehan, on his way to the plate, asked, "How's he throwing?"

Cash muttered, "Don't go up there."

Said Ryan, "It was my most overpowering no-hitter, as far as the stuff I had is concerned. Warming up in the bullpen, everything was there, and it was one of the few times I was able to take the stuff I had in the bullpen out to the mound and do it."

(cont. on page 30)

SCOREBOARD STORY. Nolan Ryan pitches to Royals' Amos Otis with two out in the ninth inning May 15. Ryan retired the K. C. hitter for a 3-0 no-hit victory.

Thanks, Jack

California	AB.	R.	H.	RBI.	E.
Pinson, lf	5	1	2	0	0
Alomar, 2b	4	1	0	0	0
Valentine, cf	4	0	1	0	0
Robinson, dh	4	0	2	0	0
Oliver, rf	3	1	1	2	0
Berry, rf	4	1	2	0	0
Gallagher, 3b	4	0	1	0	0
Spencer, 1b	4	0	1	1	0
Meoli, ss	4	0	0	0	0
Torborg, c	4	0	1	0	0
Ryan, p	0	0	0	0	0
Totals	36	3	11	3	0

Kansas City	AB.	R.	H.	RBI.	E.
Patek, ss	4	0	0	0	0
Hovley, rf	4	0	0	0	0
Otis, cf	3	0	0	0	0
Mayberry, 1b	3	0	0	0	0
Rojas, 2b	3	0	0	0	0
Kirkpatrick, dh-c	3	0	0	0	0
Piniella, lf	3	0	0	0	0
Schaal, 3b	2	0	0	0	0
Taylor, c	1	0	0	0	0
Hopkins, ph	1	0	0	0	0
Dal Canton, p	0	0	0	0	0
Garber, p	0	0	0	0	0
Totals	27	0	0	0	0

California . . . . 2 0 0   0 0 1   0 0 0—3
Kansas City . . . . 0 0 0   0 0 0   0 0 0—0

California	IP.	H.	R.	ER.	BB.	SO.
Ryan (W. 5-3)	9	0	0	0	3	12

Kansas City	IP.	H.	R.	ER.	BB.	SO.
Dal Cant'n (L. 2-2)	5⅔	8	3	3	1	0
Garber	3⅓	3	0	0	0	0

DP—Kansas City 1. LOB—California 8, Kansas City 3. HR—Oliver (4). SB—Hovley. SH—Alomar. U—Evans, Rice, Goetz and Maloney. T—2:20. A—12,205.

GAME PLAYED UNDER PROTEST

McKeon Claims Ryan Threw Illegal Pitches

Exclusive to The Times from a Staff Writer

KANSAS CITY—Jack McKeon is a swell guy—affable, pleasant, a sweetheart in victory or defeat.

There's just one thing, though. He'd like to take Nolan Ryan's no-hitter away from him.

McKeon, the Royals' manager, said after Ryan's accomplishment Tuesday night that the Angel pitcher was throwing an illegal pitch and

"but he didn't take it off the rubber. What he was doing was legal. I went out and warned him not to exaggerate it."

McKeon played the game under protest anyhow and it will be up to Cronin to decide officially. Since he will do that based on the umpire's

Please Turn to Page 6, Col. 1

RYAN GIVES ROYALS A NO-HIT PITCH, 3-0

Los Angeles Times
Sports
BUSINESS & FINANCE
CC   PART III   2†

BY RON RAPOPORT
Times Staff Writer

KANSAS CITY—The Kansas City Royals' 33-game hitting streak came to an end Tuesday night when Nolan Ryan's first no-hitter stopped them cold in a 3-0 Angel victory.

Ever since baseball people first saw Ryan's sizzling fastball, they said that if he could add some effective slow pitches, there would come a time when they would send a ball to the Hall of Fame with his name on it.

Tuesday night, before 12,205 people in Kansas City's beautiful new futuristic ballpark, it was time.

Ryan allowed only 3 baserunners,

ball that always leaves the hitters struggling for words to describe it.

"He's throwing the ball harder than any man I ever saw in my life," said John Mayberry who leads the American League in runs batted in.

"If they had a higher league," said Hal McRae, "he could be in it. As a matter of fact, he could be super in it."

"I knew he was throwing hard," added Bruce Dal Canton, the losing pitcher, "because he dug a hole a foot deep in front of the mound just shoving off."

Ryan struck out at least one batter in every inning and allowed only 2 grounders that he didn't field personally. Walks to Steve Hovley in

Only Hovley got as far as second, which he stole.

So effectively was Ryan pitching that there was really only one difficult play for the fielders behind him although there were a couple of hard-hit balls in the late innings.

The one fielding gem came with 2 out in the eighth after Schaal had walked. Pinch-hitter Gail Hopkins popped a high ball over Rudy Meoli's head that sent the rookie shortstop scrambling desperately out after it as Bobby Valentine came racing in from center.

With his back to the infield, Meoli reached out as far as he could at the last instant and came up with the ball.

I would have caught up to it or not if I hadn't. I thought I had a chance because I knew it would be in between, but if Bobby had yelled something I'm out of it. The Astroturf helped because you can really run on that turf."

Then came the ninth. Fred Patek fouled to first-baseman Jim Spencer in front of the Kansas City dugout. Steve Hovley struck out on a 2-2 pitch to become Ryan's 12th and last strikeout victim.

Enter Amos Otis, a former teammate of Ryan's when both were with the Mets.

Otis took the first pitch for a strike and then slammed a fastball hard to

track to make the catch and end the game.

"I thought it had a chance," Berry said of the final out. "But then I saw Berry sitting there and it was just a can of beans."

"I was about three feet from the wall when I caught it," said Berry. "I was afraid I was going to have to jump. In fact, I started jumping when it was hit."

And there it was, the no-hitter that sent Ryan's teammates spilling jubilantly out onto the field, the one that placed him with Clyde Wright and Bo Belinsky as Angel no-hit pitchers, the one everyone had been expecting all along.

26

California Angels

No-Hitter no. 1

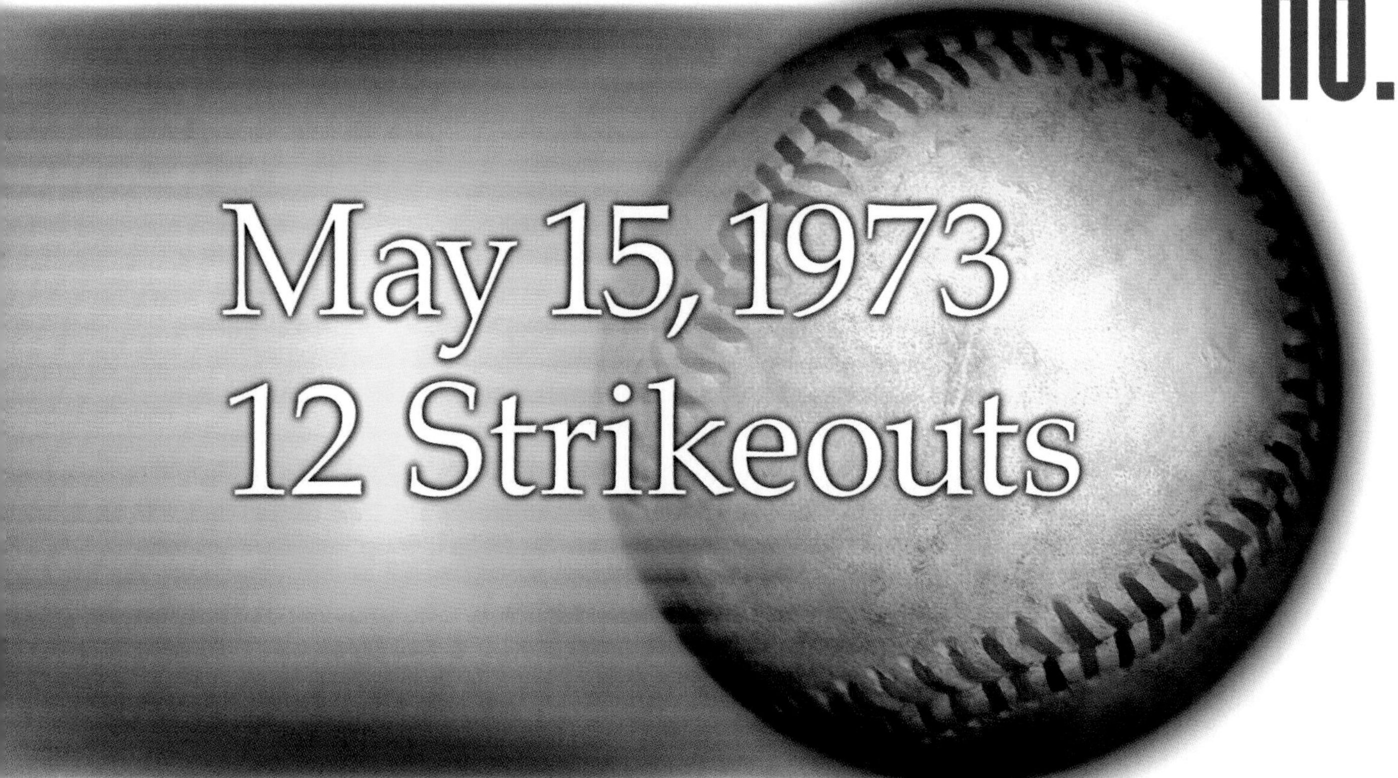

May 15, 1973
12 Strikeouts

Angels 3 - Royals 0

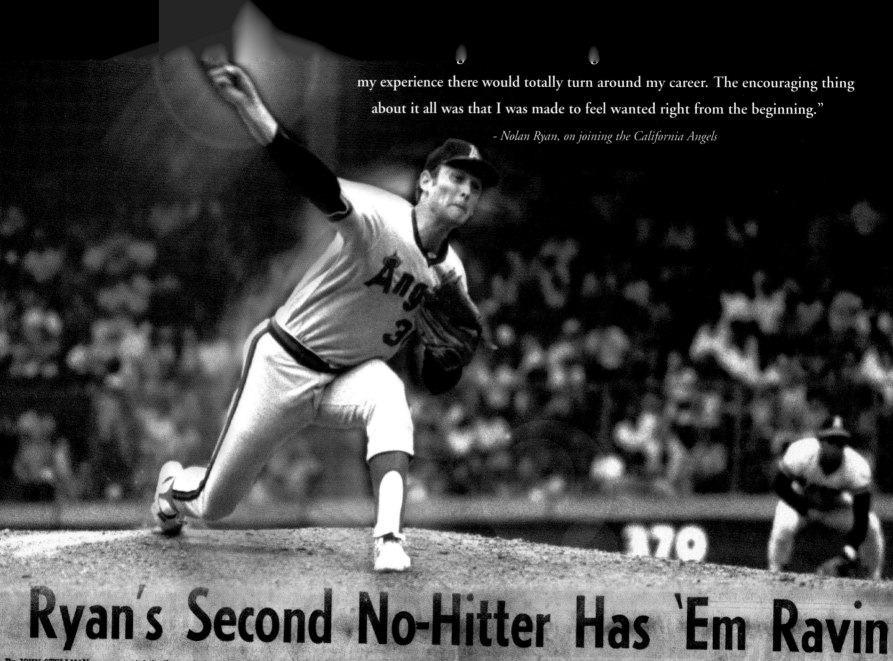

"my experience there would totally turn around my career. The encouraging thing about it all was that I was made to feel wanted right from the beginning."

- Nolan Ryan, on joining the California Angels

Ryan's Second No-Hitter Has 'Em Ravin

BY JOHN STELLMAN

I've never seen anybody that d before. When his fast ball rted coming up, there was no y anyone was going to touch

On top of that, he put his

est he's thrown it consistently for strikes." — Art Kusnyer.

"He keeps saying he needs a good second half, and I think this will get him started."— Bobby Winkles.

"That's the best stuff and the

There was one away in the ninth inning when lefthanded hitting Gates Brown sent a screaming line drive that the shortstop leaped, and clutched with both hands.

"When I saw Brown's hit, I

SPORTS

The REGISTER

gave Nolie a 1-0 advantage that he nursed into the eighth.

Then, Meoli doubled, and Kusnyer bunted to third baseman Aurelio Rodriquez. Rodriguez threw to Brinkman, now covering third. But nobody was

home two more after another walk to Ken Berry.

Ryan finally ran out to the mound, but he couldn't catch up with history.

"In the eighth inning I really

"That long eight about drove me smiled. "I was nervous than the because I'd been and I knew what

California Angels

No-Hitter no. 2

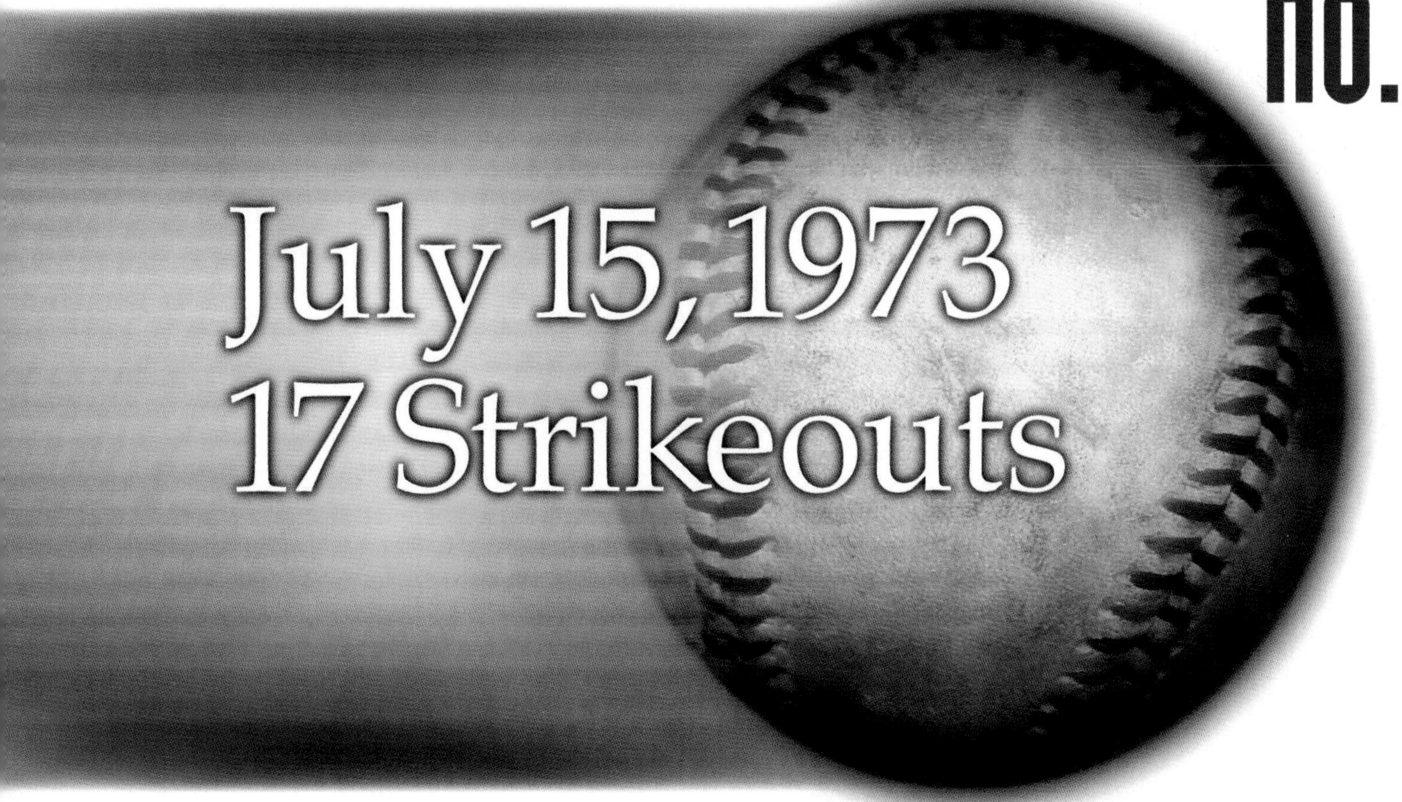

July 15, 1973
17 Strikeouts

Angels 6 - Tigers 0

(cont. from page 25)

Ryan struck out 16 through seven innings. Then the Angels scored five in the top of the eighth. Ryan lost some of his edge while sitting on the bench and missed out on a single-game strikeout record.

Cash came to the plate once more in the ninth but not with a bat. Instead he was carrying a piano leg. When umpire Ron Luciano asked Cash what he was doing, he replied, "Hell, I can't hit him with anything else."

Ryan joined Johnny Vander Meer, Allie Reynolds, Virgil Trucks and Jim Maloney as the only two pitchers to ever throw two no-hitters in one season.

Ryan came close to joining Vander Meer as the only pitcher to ever throw back-to-back no-hitters. Against the Baltimore Orioles in his next start, Ryan took a no-hitter into the eighth inning before Mark Belanger broke up the bid with a single.

"I remember specifically going out that day and trying to throw a no-hitter," Ryan said. "It's the first and only time I've ever tried to do that."

Ryan finished that season with a record of 21-16 with a 2.87 ERA. But, with the two no-hitters and the single-season strikeout record, he still finished second in the Cy Young Award voting behind Baltimore's Jim Palmer. It would be the closest he came to winning a pitcher's most coveted award.

On Aug. 12, Ryan struck out 19 batters in a nine-inning game against the Boston Red Sox to break Bob Feller's single-game American League record and tie the major league record held by Tom Seaver and Steve Carlton.

The Angels were a bad team for most of Ryan's time in California. But the victories, strikeouts and no-hitters kept coming. He was 22-16 with a 2.89 ERA and 367 strikeouts in 1974 and, in his last start of the season September 28, 1974, he threw his third no-hitter, this one coming against the Minnesota Twins.

"I don't remember much at all about that one," Ryan said. "It was the end of the season and I was just looking forward to getting home and being with my family."

There were other memorable moments that season.

On Aug. 12, Ryan struck out 19 batters in a nine-inning game against the Boston Red Sox to break Bob Feller's single-game American League record and tie the major-league record held by Tom Seaver and Steve Carlton.

It would be one of three times that year he struck out 19 in a single game, although the other two were extra-inning affairs.

Rockwell International, an electronics engineering firm, had a special treat in store for Ryan when he went out to pitch against the

100.9 mph
fastball

Chicago White Sox on Aug. 20. They introduced the forerunner of the modern radar gun, a device that could measure how fast a pitcher was throwing.

Ryan was clocked in the ninth inning at 100.9 miles per hour.

"I don't know if that was the fastest pitch I threw in the game, and I know I have thrown faster pitches in my career," Ryan said. "But that pitch stands as an all-time record."

Injuries bothered Ryan all through the 1975 season. There were a series of pulled muscles in his leg and an aching elbow that never went away. He was shut down the final five weeks of the season because of it and finally had surgery.

But he still made major league history on June 1, 1975, when he threw his fourth career no-hitter. The 1-0 victory over the Baltimore Orioles tied him with Sandy Koufax for the all-time record.

"Up to that point, breaking Sandy's strikeout record and tying his no-hitter record were the two biggest thrills of my career," Ryan said. "Nobody believed me but in that fourth no-hitter, I didn't have very good stuff. I thought I had been lucky. Only Ruth knew how much I was hurting and how unexpected the no-hitter was."

Ryan returned to health in 1976 and struck out 327 batters. In 1977, he went 19-16 with a 2.77 ERA and 341 strikeouts. He was named *The Sporting News* Pitcher of the Year but his failure to get that 20th victory in the final three weeks of the season cost him the

Cy Young Award.

But things were also looking up for the Angels. Free agency had come to baseball and Angels owner Gene Autry was an eager participant, determined more than ever to win a World Series.

He signed second baseman Bobby Grich and outfielders Don Baylor and Joe Rudi to big contracts and traded for Rod Carew. Ryan himself was given a three-year deal before the 1977 season.

Autry's generosity finally paid off in 1979. The Angels, under new manager Jim Fregosi, won their first division title, putting them in the American League Championship Series against the Baltimore Orioles. Ryan, 16-14 with a 3.59 ERA that year, faced fellow Hall of Famer Jim Palmer in Game One but left after seven innings with the game 3-3.

The Orioles went on to win that game and the series as well, denying Ryan and his teammates a trip to the World Series. Still, it was a great season for the franchise except for one small detail.

Ryan had pitched his last game for the California Angels. He was about to become a free agent and prove that indeed you can go home again.

Buzzie Bavasi was a successful baseball executive. He had

(cont. on page 38)

"Only Ruth knew"

California Angels
No-Hitter 3
no. 3

September 28, 1974
15 Strikeouts

Angels 4 - Twins 0

Ryan Hurls 4th Noooooo-Hitter

...his career, tying Ryan with ex-Dodger great Sandy Koufax as the only ones in

history to throw four no-hitters... struck out nine Sunday as... record to 9-3 for the year... four no-hitters Ryan has th... one-hitters and seven two-hit...

...Nolan Equals Koufax's All-Time Record

By CHUCK ABAIR

Everytime Nolan Ryan pitch-s you have the feeling some-ing big is going to happen.

The remarkable righthander n't disappoint the 18,492 cu-ous fans who turned up at aheim Stadium on a sunny nday afternoon by throwing fourth no-hitter of his car-r to blank Baltimore 1-0.

n doing so, he tied the major gue record held by Sandy fax, on his 100th game, and pped the Angels' five-game

anyone and he will have a per-fect game. He is only 28 and may go seven more years.

"Before the game, Billy Muf-fett said he was getting strong-er as he warmed up and was really bringing it."

Ryan, sometimes known as "the franchise," was especially pleased it was his second no-hit-ter at home. The other was 4-0 Sept. 28 a year ago against Minnesota. He previously had fired two in 1973 — 3-0 at Kan-sas City and 6-0 at Detroit

With the fans cheering on every pitch, he retired the last eight batters in order following a one-out walk and an error in the seventh.

Then Nolan responded to a

ANGEL BAROMETER

Sunday	18,492
1975 (23 dates)	377,864
1974 (23 dates)	314,243
Increase	63,261

also walked Tom Shopay. Al Bumbry, who beat out a bunt in Baltimore to break up a Ryan no-hit bid May 18, then fanned for the second time.

"I was really pleased it hap-pened at home for our fans," said Ryan about his 22nd career shutout and 20th as an Angel. "I was mainly trying to keep them from scoring."

Successive singles by Mickey Rivers, Tommy Harper and Dave Chalk

Don Baylor, who has speed and might have beaten out the same play. Singleton flied deep to left field in the eighth, but Morris Nettles caught it easily in front of the fence.

"It was a do-or-die play," commented rookie Remy. "I was shading Davis towards the bag and tried to get as much on the throw as I could."

Veteran catcher Ellie Rodri-guez, who was playing for the

tiny ball and said 'this is what I am going to be throwing.'"

"It was the best I've seen him pitch as far as getting his fast-ball, curve and changeup in good location. This was better than going 4-for-4 with a ho-mer."

Williams felt Ryan should have had a minimum three runs to work on after the Angels had managed just the single tally on eight singles and one walk

California Angels

No-Hitter 4

no. 4

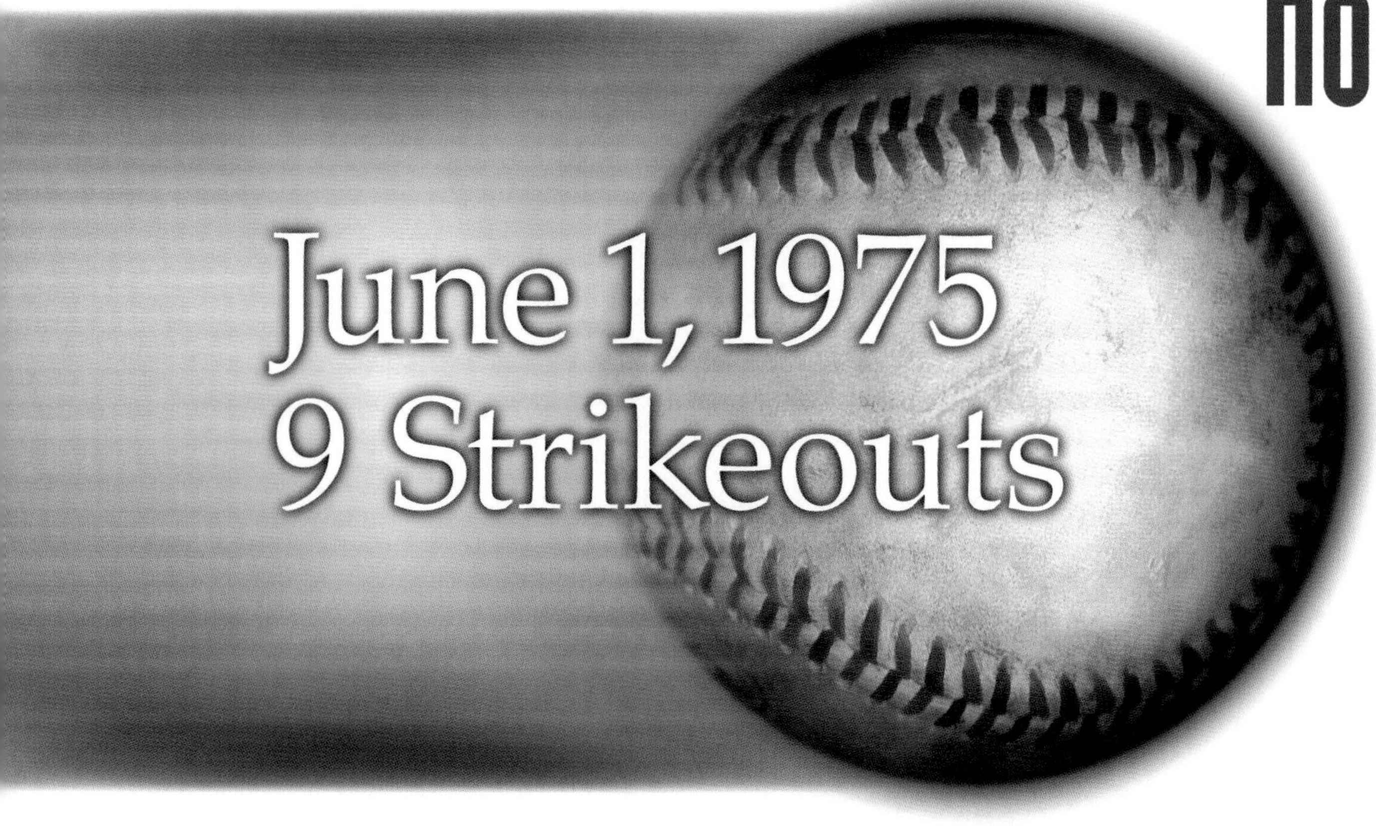

June 1, 1975
9 Strikeouts

Angels 4 - Twins 0

New York Yankees owner George Steinbrenner told Moss that Ryan was worth $1 million a year.

won a couple of World Series while general manager of the Los Angeles Dodgers and Autry hired him to do the same for the Angels. He started out well, putting together a division winner in 1979.

Then he blundered.

Ryan, who had a close relationship with Autry, wrote a letter to him before the 1979 season saying he didn't want to be a free agent and would be willing to sign a three-year extension worth $1.4 million. Bavasi declined the offer, saying they would talk after the season.

By that time, Ryan had concluded Bavasi wasn't all that interested in bringing him back. So Ryan hired an agent, Dick Moss, to handle negotiations.

New York Yankees owner George Steinbrenner told Moss that Ryan was worth $1 million a year. When Astros owner John McMullen agreed, Ryan told Moss to "make every effort to get me signed with Houston. The Astros were the only club we talked to. They had never been involved in free agency before so I really never expected to sign with them.

"But when the opportunity came up, it was like a dream come true because I would be able to live at home and be with my family."

Ryan, now 33, eventually signed a three-year deal worth $1 million per season, the first million dollar player in major league history.

"I thought that would be the last contract I ever signed," Ryan said. "I thought I would pitch three years with the Astros and that would be it. Being a power pitcher, I never thought I would last as long as I did."

$1,000,000 *per season*

Unlike his early years with the Angels, Ryan found himself on a competitive ballclub when he arrived in Houston. The Astros had won 89 games the year before and finished second in the N.L. West.

But they were also a unique team. They played their games in the Astrodome, world famous for being the first indoor stadium anywhere and the first one to use Astroturf.

The Astrodome was also a pitcher's park, so the Astros planned accordingly. They built their team around speed, pitching and defense. During Ryan's nine years on the team, they averaged 145 stolen bases per season and just 93 home runs.

Their style lended itself to close, exciting games. But it also made it tougher for Ryan to rack up the impressive win totals he did with the Angels. In those years, Ryan simply hung around until the end when the Angels finally eked out a victory.

But he was older in Houston and his complete game totals declined by the year. He would watch many victories slip away late in the game after he was finished pitching.

"That was just the type of ballclub we had," Ryan said. "But those were still the most enjoyable years I had in baseball because the ballclub was real stable and I was able to be at home. The guys from those Astros teams were probably as good a bunch of guys as I've ever played with."

McMullen's investment paid off that first year as Ryan helped

the Astros win their first division title ever before losing to the Philadelphia Phillies in the 1980 League Championship Series.

The 1981 season was a notable one for Ryan and Major League Baseball. That was the year of the 52-day players strike that started on June 12 and effectively cut the season into two halves. Under the terms of the settlement, the first-place winner in the first half of each division would play the winner of the second half.

The Los Angeles Dodgers won the first half in the N.L. West and were threatening to win the second half as well when they took the field at the Astrodome for a nationally televised game on Sept. 26. Ryan would pitch for the Astros.

"It had been six years since my last no-hitter," Ryan said. "I really thought that part of my career was over."

It wasn't. Ryan, pitching against the team that would eventually

In Ryan's fifth no-hitter, against the Dodgers, he struck out 11 and broke Sandy Koufax's record.

win the World Series, walked three, struck out 11 and did not give up a hit, the fifth no-hitter of his career. He had passed Sandy Koufax.

"That one was real special because of the circumstances," Ryan said. "It was at home in the Astrodome, where the fans have always been good to me. It was against the Los Angeles Dodgers, who had a real good ballclub. And it was during a pennant race, in a game we needed to win."

The Astros' 5-0 victory pushed them into the divisional playoff against the Dodgers. Ryan won the first game, 3-1, with a two-hit complete game performance. But the Dodgers rallied to win the series, winning Game Five over Ryan when the Astros committed three errors.

Ryan and the Astros would not reach post-season again for another five years. But the strikeout milestones were starting to pileup.

When Ryan recorded his 3,000th strikeout on July 4, 1980, against Cincinnati's Cesar Geronimo, it was evident he might break the all-time career record of 3,508, set by Hall of Famer Walter Johnson. He was in a race with Philadelphia's Steve Carlton but Ryan won on April 27, 1983, in Montreal.

Expos pinch-hitter Brad Mills was the victim, looking at a 1-2 curveball for the historic called third strike that officially anointed Ryan as the greatest strikeout pitcher of all-time.

"I think a lot of people think I really tried to strike out a lot of people and that was not the case," Ryan said. "I was just always a strikeout style of pitcher. That's what my stuff made me, that's not what I tried to become. The style of pitcher that I was, I got a lot of hitters to swing and miss.

"There were times with the Angels when I was on a roll that I went for strikeouts. I felt that with the kind of team I had behind me, if the hitter put the ball in play ... well, I had a better chance if I struck people out. But I didn't go in there with each pitch saying I'm going to throw the ball past this batter."

Ryan was 36 when he struck out Mills. He was 14-9 with a 2.98 ERA that year but with just 183 strikeouts. The years of no-hitters and leading the league in strikeouts seemed to be behind him. Most

"The style of pitcher that I was, I got a lot of hitters to swing and miss."

people expected his career to start drawing to a close.

But Ryan was changing as a pitcher. During the 1981 players' strike, Ryan finally developed a changeup, a pitch that had never really been a part of his repertoire.

"I think the changeup made my fastballs more effective," Ryan said. "On nights when I didn't have a good curve ball, it kept hitters from sitting on my fastball. That helped me pitch more innings and I struck out more people."

Ryan also mastered control. Ryan is baseball's all-time leader with 2,795 walks and he led the league in walks eight times, another major league record. In 1977, he walked 6.14 batters per nine innings.

But in 1984, that changed dramatically. Ryan walked a reason-

(cont. on page 44)

Ryan notches 5th no-hitter

Feat stands all alone in records

Related photo/page 14A
Details in Sports/page 1C

By KENNY HAND
Post Sports Reporter

John McMullen wore a smile as broad as Texas, a million-dollar smile.

"I told you he was worth it," said the Astros' chairman of the board. "I told you Nolan Ryan was worth a million. It was doomed to happen. He had to pitch another no-hitter."

Last year McMullen lavished a $1.125-million-per-year contract on free agent Ryan, the 34-year-old Alvin rancher. There were some critics, especially when Ryan was hamstrung by injuries all year and won only 11 games.

Already this season he's 10-5, including 50 days obliterated by the ball strike. "How could I not pay

Houston Astros
No-Hitter 5
no. 5

September 26, 1981
11 Strikeouts

Astros 5 - Dodgers 0

(cont. from page 41)

able 3.38 batters per nine innings. By cutting down the number of walks, Ryan also reduced the number of pitches he threw in a game and lessened the wear-and-tear on his arm.

Finally there was his legendary work ethic. Dr. Gene Coleman, who worked with the Astros, designed a training program for Ryan and he would follow it religiously year-round. By doing so, he would keep his career going long beyond what anybody expected.

Still, 1986 was almost the end of the line for Ryan. It was a glorious year, but also one filled with pain, especially in his right elbow. Ryan started feeling the pain in spring training and it never subsided.

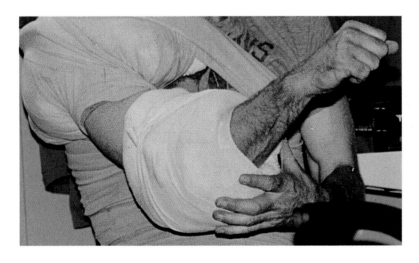

He twice had to go on the disabled list.

He was 12-8 with a 3.34 ERA but struck out only 194 batters. On Sept. 24, he beat the Giants, 6-0, striking out 12 in eight innings,

Ryan was 39 and his elbow ached.

and the Astros clinched a tie for the division championship. The next day teammate Mike Scott, the Cy Young winner that year, pitched a no-hitter and the Astros were back in the playoffs, this time against the New York Mets.

The Mets, a powerful ballclub led by Dwight Gooden and Darryl Strawberry, had won 108 games that year. But the two teams split the first four games of the best-of-seven series when Ryan and Gooden met in Game Five on Oct. 14 at Shea Stadium.

Ryan was 39 and his elbow ached. Gooden was 21 and in the best shape of his career. The matchup was billed as "The New Nolan Ryan vs. The Old Nolan Ryan." It was a classic.

Ryan allowed two hits, including a home run to Strawberry, in nine innings. He struck out 12. His elbow screamed at him every step of the way but he blocked out the pain.

Gooden was just as good though, allowing one run in 10 innings. The game went on after the two aces were pulled and the Mets won in 12 innings, 2-1.

Afterwards, Scott marveled at Ryan's courage, saying, "That is the best game I've ever seen pitched. It was the best, that's all. The best. It was the game, the situation, the closeness of it all. I've never seen a better game. Not even my own no-hitter."

The Mets won Game Six and advanced to the World Series. Ryan went back to Alvin and pondered his future. The elbow was enough of a concern that doctors suggested a major operation. Ryan declined. He would rest through the winter and see how it felt in spring training.

Miraculously, the pain was gone when spring training rolled around. Ryan was throwing free and easy again and, at age 40, instead of retiring, he became a dominating pitcher again.

Ryan led the National League that year with both 270 strikeouts and a 2.76 ERA. Yet he finished with a disappointing 8-16 record, a combination of poor relief pitching, the Astros anemic offense and a front-office mandated 110-pitch limit. Often Ryan would leave the game with a lead after 110 pitches and watch as the bullpen squandered the game away.

"I said all year Nolan's record should've been turned around," Astros manager Hal Lanier said. "With his final record at 8-16, that was not true anymore. I don't think anyone would've said that he

should've been 16-8. Any knowledgeable baseball man, looking at his numbers, would say this pitcher should have 20 wins.

"If you looked at it that way, Nolan would have been the hands-down winner of the Cy Young Award."

Ryan's luck improved a little in 1988. He was 12-11 with a 3.52 ERA and he led the league in strikeouts again with 228. He also just missed a no-hitter against the Philadelphia Phillies when Mike Schmidt singled with one out in the ninth.

However, at age 41, Ryan felt the time was approaching when he would finally retire. He was still making $1 million per season but all through his years with the Astros, he never saw the need for a raise. He enjoyed pitching for the Astros, he enjoyed being close to home and he was ready to pitch for that amount one more time.

"I felt 1989 would be my last season and I would retire as an Astro," Ryan said.

He was wrong. The Legend of Nolan Ryan was about to reach new heights that not even he could have ever foreseen in his wildest dreams. But he would be wearing a new uniform.

The ad was designed to sell Astros season-tickets and it included a photo of Ryan being carried off the field by his teammates. He had just pitched his fifth no-hitter and the sales pitch read: DON'T MISS THE NEXT NO-HITTER.

The irony of the slogan would be remembered nine years later when the Astros did just that. They missed Ryan's next no-hitter.

When Ryan met with the Astros to discuss his 1989 contract he was shocked to find out John McMullen wanted to cut his salary 20 percent. Ryan was stunned, then infuriated. He called Dick Moss, his agent, and decided to go back out on the free agent market.

Autry wanted him back with the Angels. The San Francisco Giants wanted him badly. So too did the Texas Rangers and their interest intrigued Ryan. He was leaning toward returning to the Angels because of his close friendship with Autry but the Rangers situation appealed to him as well because of his family.

The Rangers weren't the Astros but they were still in Texas and it meant not having to uproot his family. When the four teams made their final offers, Ryan chose the Rangers.

Ryan explained his decision by saying, "I really wanted to stay in Texas. I'm certainly disappointed the Houston situation didn't work

out. Houston is my home ... the overriding factor was what I felt was best for myself and my family."

Ryan agreed to a one-year contract worth $1.8 million with an option at $1.4 million for 1990. But that was a moot point as far as Ryan was concerned. He still believed 1989 would be his final season.

The Rangers were a franchise in transition under Tom Grieve and manager Bobby Valentine. They had lost 99 games in 1985 but an influx of exciting young talent and Valentine's provocative managerial style brought about a stunning turn-around in 1986. They went 87-75 and battled the Angels down to the final weeks of the season in the A.L. West before finishing second.

But that thrilling season was followed by two sixth-place finishes. The turnaround had hit a lull and new blood was needed. The Rangers traded for second baseman Julio Franco and first baseman Rafael Palmeiro as well as signing Ryan.

There were still some doubts. Ryan was 42 and had not won more than 12 games in a season since 1982. A calf muscle problem in spring training created further doubt.

There was little reason to believe Ryan was about to embark on one of the most remarkable seasons of his career. Given his age, it would also have to rank as one of the most remarkable ever for any player in history.

The first indication came in his second start. Ryan took a no-hitter into the eighth inning against the Mil-waukee Brewers before Terry Francona singled to left. In his fourth start against the Toronto Blue Jays, Ryan took a no-hitter into the ninth be-fore giving up a one-out triple to Nelson Liriano.

> There was little reason to believe Ryan was about to embark on one of the most remarkable seasons of his career. Given his age, it would also have to rank as one of the most remarkable ever for any player in history.

The Rangers won that game, 4-1, but Ryan admitted afterward, "I'm more disappointed than pleased about winning the ballgame. I generally just go out and try and win the ballgame, but to get to that point, it's disappointing not to get the no-hitter."

Ryan was only getting started. His next start was just as memo-rable, a head-to-head matchup with Roger Clemens and the Boston Red Sox on a Sunday afternoon at Arlington Stadium.

Pitching in front of a sellout crowd of 40,429, the two were at their best. But Ryan was just a little bit better, prevailing 2-1 when Palmeiro hit a two-run homer off Clemens in the eighth.

"I think the fans got their money's worth," Ryan said.

So did the 37,867 fans who showed up at Anaheim Stadium on July 6 to see the Rangers play the California Angels. Ryan pitched for the Rangers that day, his first appearance at Anaheim Stadium since leaving the Angels as a free agent after the 1979 season.

He received three separate standing ovations, the first and loudest when he walked in from the bullpen to start the game. Ryan then went out and beat the Angels, 3-0.

"It was a special feeling," Ryan said. "Coming out of the bullpen, I don't think I've ever had a reception like that. It was one of the highlights of my career. I'll always remember it."

Ryan was back at Anaheim Stadium a week later as a member of the American League All-Star team, the eighth and last time he was selected to play in the mid-Summer Classic. He pitched two scoreless innings and was the winning pitcher in the American League's 5-3 victory.

He was 10-4 with a 2.91 ERA but another milestone was looming over the horizon. Ryan had started the season with 4,775 career strikeouts and it was now obvious that sometime in August he would reach the 5,000 mark.

"I remember the night I struck out No. 4,000, somebody asked about 5,000. They said it jokingly but I thought to myself, Lord help me there is no way. I never thought I could get 5,000 strikeouts."

He did, on the memorable night of Aug. 22, 1989, pitching against the Oakland Athletics before 42,869 fans at Arlington

Commissioner Bart Giamatti and the A's Rickey Henderson congratulate Ryan after his 5,000th strikeout.

Stadium. Future Hall of Famer Rickey Henderson was the victim when he swung and missed at a full-count fastball.

Light bulbs popped all over the ballpark as the crowd, which included Commissioner Bart Giamatti, stood to give him a sustained standing ovation. All eight teammates in the field, including the three outfielders, jogged to the mound to offer congratulations. A message from President Bush was displayed on the giant video board.

It was a magic moment at Arlington Stadium.

"If you asked me to give the special moments of my career, obviously the 5,000th strikeout would be one," Ryan said. "There was a

> **Future Hall of Famer Rickey Henderson was the victim when he swung and missed at a full-count fastball.**

lot of electricity in the air and the fan involvement and the buildup, people getting so much involved."

Ryan finished the season with still one more memorable performance at Anaheim Stadium, pitching a three-hit shutout in a 2-0 victory. He was 16-10 with a 3.20 ERA. He also struck out 13, giving him 301 for the season, an incredible feat given his age.

The next day, the last day of the season, Ryan announced that

1989 would not be his last. He had shown he could still be an effective pitcher and people still came to the park thinking they might see the next no-hitter.

Ryan didn't think it would come on June 11, 1990, against the defending world champion Athletics. He had just spent three weeks on the disabled list because of a bad back and this was only his second start since then. The pain had not completely subsided.

"I remember when I was warming up in the bullpen that my back was still bothering me and so I was just hoping to give us six or seven good innings," Ryan said. "Again, a no-hitter was the farthest thing from my mind."

That changed as the game progressed until, after two walks and 14 strikeouts, Oakland's Willie Randolph hit a lazy fly ball to right. Ruben Sierra made the catch in foul territory and Ryan, at 43, had

(cont. on page 54)

"I was concerned with my back problems and I said, 'Well, I'll just go seven innings.' Then I got through seven and decided I'm not going to give in to it because I just need six more outs. This no-hitter comes so late in my career that it makes it very special."

-Nolan Ryan, on his sixth no-hitter

Texas Rangers
No-Hitter no.6

June 11, 1990
14 Strikeouts

Rangers 5 - A's 0

SPORTS

News & Scores

Ryan runs no-hit count to

**Ed
Fowler**

Fans stay late, seek souvenirs

Associated Press

be tough no tail

Ky. — With the Ken-
y record of 1:59 2-5, set
iat in 1973, in no appar-
s of horse flesh may not
r's event as one for the
quine psychology, on the
eaven already.
and a herd of pretend-
or Saturday afternoon.
d, Excavate and Meadow
the wayside en route to
them victims of injury.
ded year, horse head-
ar Derby Week diver-
on's weak field, it's more
uleps.
on't spend the entire
alogue with four-legged
s fail to remember how
ing this is. We tend to
ication of psychobabble
ud for a collapse of con-
ng for a midlife crisis.
orance, we vow to do our
to snicker as we under-
e most telling disclo-
ding the competitors'

o tail. Well, he has a
mp, something like what
auzer who hasn't been
a Cadet wasn't clipped,
ply born *sans* tail.
the trauma deformity
ans and of the heroic ef-
o overcome their handi-
servers on the scene spec-
s emotional state in view
amer.

ARLINGTON — Nolan Ryan's seventh no-hitter was a lucky number
Wednesday for a roaring crowd that
watched the pitcher's first such feat
at Arlington Stadium.
"It was the nicest present I've ever
gotten in baseball," said Eddie
Chiles, former Rangers chairman of
the board. "It was just wonderful it
was Nolan Ryan."
Fans were still milling around the
stadium a half-hour after the game
ended. They searched garbage cans
for programs, ticket stubs and other
paraphernalia.
Mike McCuen and his 11-year-old
son, Charlie, had collected about 50
ticket stubs and were checking trash
cans for more.
McCuen, 38, of Arlington said he
lost his program.
But "these all will be worth a lot of
money," said McCuen, who surprised
his son by purchasing tickets for
second-row box seats Wednesday
morning.
"I think Nolan Ryan is the best
pitcher in the world," said Charlie
McCuen. "He's just broken so many
records.
"Ryan is a great role model. He
carries through; he's not a quitter,"
the boy said.
The elder McCuen said he has been
interested in the 44-year-old Ryan
since he saw the first game Ryan
pitched as a member of the Texas
Rangers.
"He's a down-home-type person.

Son say dad had 'the loo

By DAVID BARRON
Houston Chronicle

He was just a fuzzy
color television screer
could sense what wa
happen.
Art Howe and Craig
Pittsburgh, Alan Ashby
Reid Ryan in Austin
could see Nolan Rya

Ryan's no-h

1. **May 15, 1973** — At K
   Angels 3, Royals 0. 12
2. **July 15, 1973** — At
   gels 6, Tigers 0. 17 stri
3. **Sept. 28, 1974** — A
   Angels 4, Twins 0. 15 s
4. **June 1, 1975** — A
   Angels 1, Orioles 0. 9 s
5. **Sept. 26, 1981** — A
   Astros 5, Dodgers 0. 11
6. **June 11, 1990** —
   Rangers 5, Athletics 0.
   outs.
7. **May 1, 1991** — A
   Rangers 3, Blue Jays
   outs.

special combination o
and power that had ca
six no-hitters and co
given night, carry hin
And Wednesday n
the Toronto Blue Jay
Reid Ryan, son of
Rangers pitcher and
itcher on the Univer

snubbed Sea Cadet

Texas Rangers
No-Hitter no.7

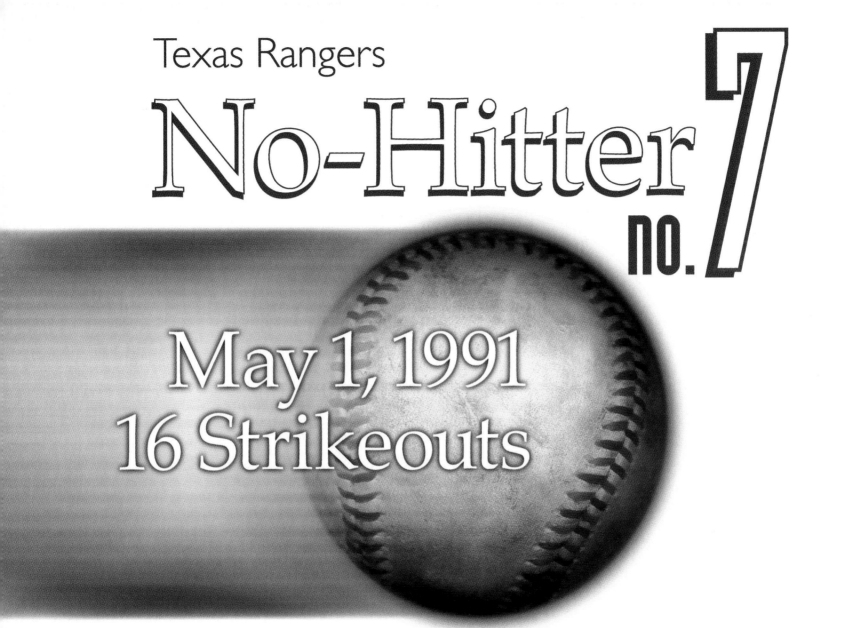

May 1, 1991
16 Strikeouts

Rangers 3 - Blue Jays 0

(cont. from page 49)

become the oldest pitcher to ever throw a no-hitter.

Two months later, Ryan made history again when he earned his 300th career victory, beating the Milwaukee Brewers. He was the 20th pitcher to reach that special plateau, a feat that all but clinched his eventual election into the Hall of Fame. He also finished the

Ryan threw his 7th no-hitter against Toronto on May 1, 1991.

season with 232 strikeouts, marking the 11th and last time he would ever lead the league in his specialty.

He still struck out 203 batters in 1991 but twice went on the disabled list with shoulder problems. The injuries were starting to mount up.

Still, there was some magic in the arm. The Rangers celebrated Arlington Appreciation Night on May 1 and Ryan, pitching against the Toronto Blue Jays, made it an extra special night by throwing his seventh career no-hitter. It came on the same day that Rickey Henderson broke Lou Brock's all-time stolen base record.

"That one was special because it came at home," Ryan said. "The fans in Arlington always treated me great, so to throw a no-hitter for them was a special feeling, again one of the highlights of my career."

But Ryan was running out of miracles. He was 5-9 with a 3.72 ERA in 1992, his fewest wins since his rookie year. He missed over a month because of injuries but he also struck out 157 in 157 innings.

Ryan announced before the 1993 season that this would be it. He was honored wherever he went but pitching became a struggle. Injuries limited him to 13 starts, his fewest since 1969. Again he won just five games. But he went down fighting in perhaps one of the strangest episodes of his career.

He was pitching against the Chicago White Sox on Aug. 4. The White Sox were leading, 2-0, in the third when Robin Ventura came to bat and took a fastball from Ryan in the shoulder.

The White Sox 27-year-old third baseman took a couple steps toward first, then charged the mound where a 46-year-old pitcher was waiting for him. Ryan grabbed Ventura in a headlock and smacked him with five uppercuts before players on both teams swarmed over them.

"Self preservation is all that goes through your mind when something like that happens," said Ryan, who denied Ventura's assertion he was throwing at him.

It was Ryan's last big moment.

The end came on Sept. 22, pitching against the Seattle Mariners.

He allowed five runs in the first inning, including a grand slam to Dann Howitt. Then, on a 1-1 pitch to Dave Magadan, he tore the ulnar collateral ligament in his elbow.

He knew his career was over. He walked off the mound, doffed his cap one more time to the crowd, and disappeared into the clubhouse.

It was not how a legend is supposed to come to an end but perhaps Oakland pitcher Dennis Eckersley, another future Hall of Famer, was right when he heard the news.

"I guess it took something that serious to end it," Eckersley said. "It's almost like he had to have his arm ripped off to stop pitching."

Rangers general manager Tom Grieve summed it up better than anybody.

"There's no way to overestimate or overstate what he's meant to this franchise," Grieve said. "He was not the only star we had. There was Ruben Sierra, Juan Gonzalez, Pudge Rodriguez, Kevin Brown, a lot of good players to look at.

"But as far as impact on the Rangers and the ability to gain credibility with the fans, there was no one like Nolan. He was also a superb pitcher. He achieved milestones that are mind-boggling, things that will never happen again."

Robin Ventura's charging
e mound against Ryan in
92 will forever be a part
baseball folklore.

5,714

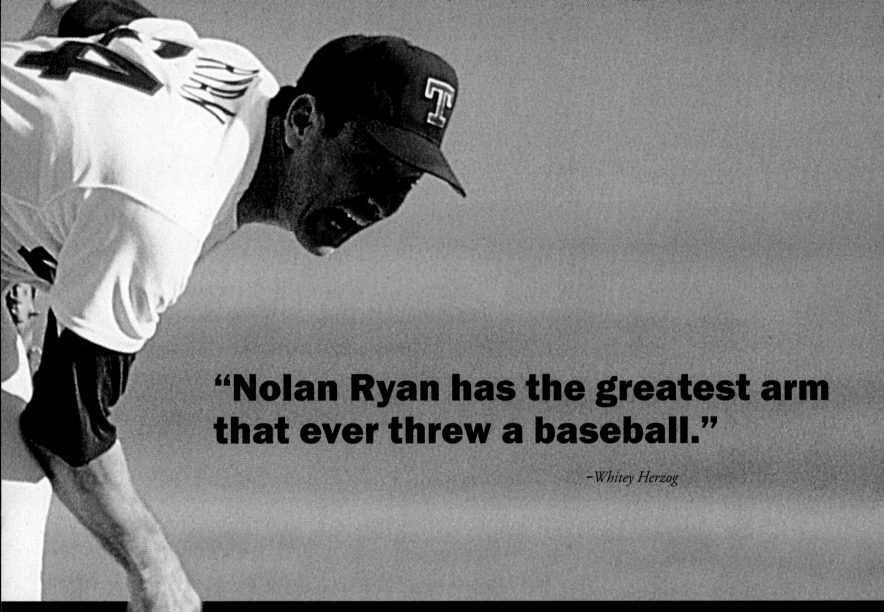

"Nolan Ryan has the greatest arm that ever threw a baseball."

–Whitey Herzog

STRIKEOUTS

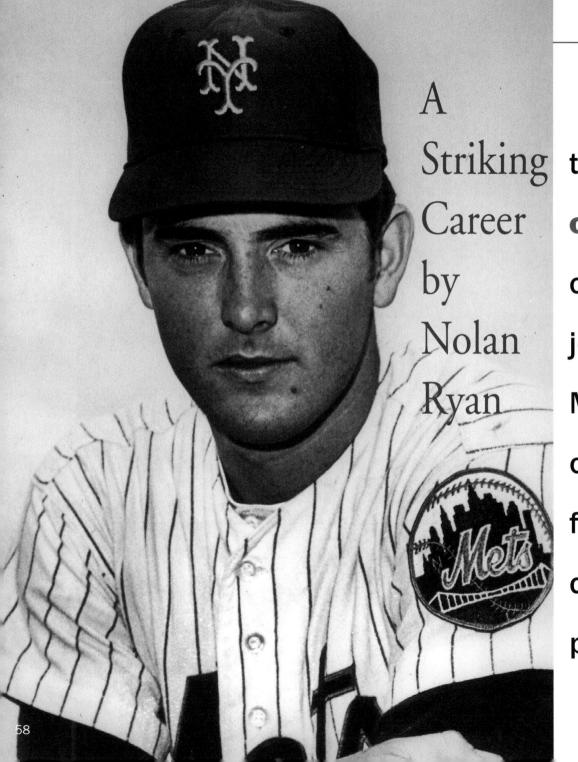

A Striking Career by Nolan Ryan

I can honestly say that making the **Hall of Fame** was not one of my goals when I joined the New York Mets in 1966. **My** obsession was to last four seasons, so I could qualify for the pension plan.

I might have quit after two, but by then I had married my high school sweetheart Ruth and I wasn't nearly so homesick. I was making $7,500 a year, and had to take out a loan to go to spring training. **But Ruth convinced me that if I went back to Alvin – and the job that was open at the hardware store – I'd always wonder if I might have made it as a big league pitcher.**

The truth is, I would have been happy selling hardware, but I guess I can say Ruth was right. But I don't think I ever gave the Hall of Fame a thought during my first sixteen years, even after I had pitched five no-hitters and broken a few strikeout records. Don

Sutton brought it up one day in 1981, when we were teammates with the Houston Astros. He was thinking about his own career, not mine.

When Sutton left the Dodgers and came to Houston, he had already mapped out the rest of his career, something that was alien to me. When he notched his 250th win, he said something like, "Well, only fifty more to go."

I asked him what he meant and he said there wasn't a 300-game winner who hadn't been elected to the Hall of Fame. So here we are, with Sutton having arrived a year before me. He may have been the best finesse pitcher I ever saw, the one least likely to give a hitter something decent to chase. He gave them crumbs. And what were the odds that both of us would finish with a total of 324 wins,

tied for 12th on the all-time list?

I rank Sutton with Pete Rose as a player who took less than prime physical ability and wasted nothing. Everything went into the blender.

What I have come to understand, in the last few years, is that there are many roads to Cooperstown. One of the neat

things about going in with the Class of '99 is that I faced all three of the hitters. As a

One of the neat things about going in with the Class of 99' is that I faced all three of the hitters.

youngster with the Mets and a little bit with the Angels, I faced Orlando Cepeda, who had his big years with the

Giants but finished with Boston and Kansas City. He was one of the premier power hitters of his time.

I saw George Brett and Robin Yount come into the league as rookies, and develop into two of the finest hitters

in the game. I hated to see Brett come to bat with a runner on third. He didn't strike out often and went with the

pitch wherever I threw it. I preferred going up against the free swingers.

When Robin broke in, at 19, he choked up and was a singles hitter. He developed into a run producer with alley to alley power.

It was against Robin's team, in Milwaukee, that I won my 300th game in August of 1990. The final score was

11-to-3, which is a little deceiving. I struck out eight, allowed six hits, threw 146 pitches and left the game in the

eighth with a 5-to-3 lead and the tying runs on base.

Three Texas errors had given the game some unwanted suspense, but my teammates came back with six in the

ninth. Julio Franco tied a ribbon around the win with a grand slam homer.

Most amazing of all, to me, was the standing ovation I got from a standing-room crowd of 57,097 fans,

"NO-LAN
NO-LAN
NO-LAN"

Milwaukee's largest of the season. I walked off the field with the chant echoing in my ears, "NO-LAN, NO-LAN, NO-LAN" in a stadium where we were the enemy.

It was fitting that we won by eight runs and I had to sweat out every pitch. But that was fine. I don't remember winning on any forfeits during my career. I pitched for teams that mostly had to scratch for runs, and I became a better pitcher because of it.

A writer once summed up my fortunes in this way: "It was as if God had given him the arm, the durable body, the work habits that would embarrass a Korean rice farmer, and then said, 'That's it, babe. Make your own breaks.'"

I have no complaints. My base-
ball journey consisted of four stages, in four cities, and it turned out to be one terrific trail ride. The Mets wanted to turn me into a relief pitcher, but doubted that I would ever learn to throw strikes. Still, I pitched for a World Series team, the Miracle Mets of 1969.

ADDENDUM NO. ONE
TO
UNIFORM PLAYER'S CONTRACT
BETWEEN
HOUSTON ASTROS BASEBALL CLUB
AND
LYNN NOLAN RYAN

This Addendum is attached to and made a part of the Uniform Player's Contract between the Houston Astros Baseball Club and L. Nolan Ryan, dated November 13, 1979, and shall be deemed to amend and modify any other provisions, rules or regulations inconsistent herewith.

A.   PAYMENT

1. **Signing Bonus.** Player shall become entitled to a bonus in the amount of $250,000 by executing this Contract, payable on January 2, 1980.

2. **Salary.** During each of the four years covered by this Contract, 1980 through 1983, Player shall be paid an annual salary of $1,000,000. Annual salary shall be paid quarterly at the end of each quarter, in four equal installments of $250,000. Player, however, shall have the right to designate different terms for salary payments, provided such terms do not (1) increase the Club's costs, (2) change the Club's tax deductibility posture or (3) create an unreasonable administrative burden. The provisions of Section B below shall apply to 1980, 1981 and 1982 salary, but shall not apply to 1983 salary.

3. **Deferred Payment.** During the first year of Player's retirement as an active player, he shall be paid the sum of $250,000, payable quarterly at the end of each quarter, in four equal installments of $62,500. Player agrees to perform, during said year, public relations services as may reasonably be requested by Club.

B.   GUARANTY OF PAYMENT

1. Regardless of any provision herein to the contrary (except as set forth in the last sentence of Section A.2 above), all compensation and benefits payable to Player shall be paid in any event, provided Player does not arbitrarily refuse to render his professional services. It is the intent and understanding of the parties that this entire Contract shall be a guaranteed contract despite any inability of Player to exhibit sufficient skill or competitive ability, and despite any mental or physical handicap or injury or death. In the event of Player's death, all payments guaranteed under this Contract shall be payable by Club to Player's estate (or to a designee of Player if Player has so authorized in writing) in accordance with the schedule of payments specified herein. Should, during the term of this Contract, Player arbitrarily refuse to render his professional services,

This Contract shall not be assigned or assignable to any other Club without the prior written consent of Player. Should, however, Club desire to assign this Contract to another Club, Player agrees that he will give serious consideration to Club's request that he give his consent to assignment.

In Witness Whereof, Club and Player have signed this Addendum on this 13th day of November, 1979.

L. Nolan Ryan   _for the Houston Astros Baseball Club_

I spent eight years with the California Angels, learned how to pitch, established myself as a starter and threw four no-hitters. I also got to work for one of the kindest men who ever lived, Gene Autry.

When I signed as a free agent with the Astros, I became the first million-dollar player, and the media laughed when I said that in two or three years that salary would not seem special. In Houston I was looked on as a kid from the neighborhood, and I was able to drive to the Astrodome from my home in Alvin in 30 minutes, in a pickup truck. I added my fifth no-hitter, broke Walter Johnson's career strikeout record and reached the league championship series twice. We kept the nucleus of that team together for nine years, about 15 of us, and I developed some tight friendships.

I was heartsick when it turned out that I would not finish my career with the Astros, but playing for the Rangers turned out to be the cherry on top. I expected to pitch one season, and stretched it to five, and that enabled me to achieve some things I never imagined:

300 wins, 5,000 strikeouts, my sixth and seventh no-hitters. I was 44 years old when I got the last one.

When I walked into my first major league clubhouse in early September of 1966, the scene actually startled me. I was nineteen, with high school and a year of minor league ball behind me, and I had never seen players smoking cigars.

That was about all they were doing – that and playing cards and answering their fan mail by sailing unopened letters into the nearest trash can. These were the New York Mets, the last of the lovable, comical, pie-in-the-face Mets. I say this with no disrespect. It was as if someone had taken a truck to a union hall and picked up a load of day workers.

Don't get me wrong. Several of them had been solid big leaguers, even famous. But now they were punching the clock, finishing out careers that had flourished somewhere else. The others in the room were kids like me, up from one of the farm clubs, a preview of coming attractions.

From that clubhouse, two of us made it to the Hall of Fame, Tom Seaver and me. So did the manager, Gil Hodges, who had been one of the Boys of Summer in Brooklyn.

Gil made a commitment to stick with us, the kids, and suddenly it was 1969, the year the Mets became truly amazing. I felt lucky to be there. I still do. The Mets had finished last or next to last every year of their existence. But we came from nine and a half games behind the Cubs in August, then stunned a great Baltimore team – Frank Robinson, Brooks Robinson, Boog Powell, Davey Johnson, that crowd - in the World Series. Our scouts kept saying, Don't throw this and don't throw that." Finally, Jerry Koosman said, "Well, what the hell do we throw these guys?"

Ryan, pitching as a reliever in Game 3 of the 1969 World Series, led the Mets to a 5-0 win over Baltimore.

We never did get an answer. But the Mets were the new lullaby of Broadway. All during the Series, we were laughing and having a good time, and the Orioles were getting tighter and tighter. We got great pitching. Little Al Weis hit a homer. Ron Swoboda made two circus catches. We lost the opener, swept the last four. Yes, we had angels on our shoulders.

That was a team thrill, maybe the biggest of my career, until now. **When you get voted into the Hall of Fame, you take every teammate you ever had with you. And some you played against.** I admire Ted Williams for speaking out on behalf of Shoeless Joe Jackson, banned for life after being tainted by the Black Sox scandal of 1919. That was 80 years ago. The evidence favors Shoeless Joe and so does Ted Williams. I don't argue with the last man to bat .400.

In my mind, Pete Rose is another who deserves to be in the Hall. I saw Pete play the game. I saw him serve his time. He ought to be honored for what he accomplished as a player.

Of course, I may be biased. Pete and I had a nice rivalry, one that went to the core of the game, to the duel between the batter and the pitcher. I don't recall many moments as intense as the day in Philadelphia when Pete tried to break the National League record for career hits – on his way to Ty Cobb's lifetime mark.

Stan Musial, who held the record, was in the stands. To make matters more interesting, Rose had projected when he would break

pete rose • outfield

"There wasn't a pitcher more feared in his era than Nolan Ryan."

- Pete Rose

Reproduced with permission © Topps Company. Inc.

Then he turned around and saluted me. That was one of the highest compliments I ever received, in all of my 27 seasons.

the record, and against which pitcher – me. He wasn't being cute. He had checked out the schedule, added up how many hits he should have by what date, and saw that the Phillies would be playing at home against the Astros (he had left the Reds after the 1978 season). That was Pete.

I knew what a competitor he was and how hard he was to strike out. But as much as he was focused on getting the record, I was focused on not letting him do it. In his first at-bat, he hit a soft liner over short for the hit that tied Musial. Then I struck him out the next three times.

That whole scenario was one of the most meaningful moments of my career. It was as one-on-one as baseball can get. After he struck out the third time, Pete broke his bat on the ground walking back to the dugout. Then he turned around and saluted me. That was one of the highest compliments I ever received, in all of my 27 seasons.

My career didn't exactly get cut short. I pitched until I was 46 and, sure, pride had something to do with it. But the fact is, I still had my fastball and could still kick it up to 95 on the radar gun. To the very end, I was giving my team innings, keeping my team in the game, giving us a chance to win.

And when people look at my plaque, hanging in the Hall of Fame, I hope that is what they will remember.

— Nolan Ryan

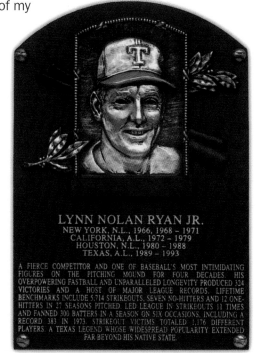

LYNN NOLAN RYAN JR.
NEW YORK, N.L., 1966, 1968 – 1971
CALIFORNIA, A.L., 1972 – 1979
HOUSTON, N.L., 1980 – 1988
TEXAS, A.L., 1989 – 1993

A FIERCE COMPETITOR AND ONE OF BASEBALL'S MOST INTIMIDATING FIGURES ON THE PITCHING MOUND FOR FOUR DECADES. HIS OVERPOWERING FASTBALL AND UNPARALLELED LONGEVITY PRODUCED 324 VICTORIES AND A HOST OF MAJOR LEAGUE RECORDS. LIFETIME BENCHMARKS INCLUDE 5,714 STRIKEOUTS, SEVEN NO-HITTERS AND 12 ONE-HITTERS IN 27 SEASONS PITCHED. LED LEAGUE IN STRIKEOUTS 11 TIMES AND FANNED 300 BATTERS IN A SEASON ON SIX OCCASIONS, INCLUDING A RECORD 383 IN 1973. STRIKEOUT VICTIMS TOTALED 1,176 DIFFERENT PLAYERS. A TEXAS LEGEND WHOSE WIDESPREAD POPULARITY EXTENDED FAR BEYOND HIS NATIVE STATE.

Questions *and* Answers

with Nolan Ryan

Q

Who was your *greatest* influence?

A

I inherited my work ethic from my father, who held two jobs for as long as I was growing up. He worked for an

oil company during the day and at night he was a distributor for *The Houston Post.* As soon as I was old enough to help him,

we would get up at 1 a.m. to roll the papers, then I'd toss them out the car window to 1,500 homes over a 55-mile route.

At 5, I'd drop back into bed to sleep another hour or two before school. If a customer said they didn't get their paper,

my dad didn't argue. We jumped back in the car and dropped one off as quickly as possible.

He was **Lynn Nolan Ryan, Sr.,** and he taught me to be responsible.

(He died in 1970, a year after I pitched in the World Series for the Mets.)

Tom Seaver was the first friend I had on the Mets. He was the Rookie of the Year the season before I got there.

Tom changed the attitude on the team. He didn't thinking losing was funny or cute. He was driven, goal-oriented, polished.

I watched the way he conducted himself on and off the field, always with class. He became a role model for me.

Someone who helped an awful lot was Tom Morgan, the pitching coach with the Angels.

Morgan believed in me, and when I came over from the Mets my confidence was shaky.

He helped me probably as much as anybody at any time in my career.

The first three years with the Angels, I pitched right at 1,000 innings and I think that was a real key to my success.

Ryan's disciplined training regimen allowed him to pitch for a major-league record 27 seasons.

Q

The first time you wore a jersey—
what was that like?

As a kid, to get your hat to start with and you're on a team for the first time,

you have a great feeling. Then your game finally rolls around after two or three weeks of practice.

All kids probably put on their uniform six hours before the game and bug their parents to

get to the ballpark three or four hours before you are supposed to ... that's just the excitement and anticipation of it.

I still remember that.

The glove we have in the display in Alvin, is the first glove

I ever had that was my very own. I remember going to Alvin Hardware with my dad, as the last of six kids,

to pick out for the first time anything new for myself, and it's not a hand-me-down.

I could pick out any glove I wanted. That was a big experience because it was the first time that had ever happened.

I go by that display and see the glove and that's one of the things I think about.

That was a real high spot in my life.

It's so old you can't even read the numbers, but you can read my name where

I burned it in with a wood burning set to make sure no one would get away with it.

Ryan's first baseball glove.

Q

Who were *your heroes?*

A

In rural Texas, our exposure to Major League Baseball was very limited. It was what you got out of newspapers
or on St. Louis Cardinals broadcasts or the *Game of the Week,* once that started. I was a Mickey Mantle fan. Most kids are at-
tracted to making the great catch or hitting home runs and I was no different, until I started pitching in high school.
Then I was a Sandy Koufax fan. I remember taking Ruth to old Colt Stadium in Houston, when we were still in high school.
My friend's aunt got the tickets.
Ruth and I were in a box seat on the front row. The pitchers warmed up in front of the dugout then.
They didn't go down to the bullpen. The club had put down a home plate right in front of the dugout. Ruth couldn't
understand why I was so excited. I really believe Sandy Koufax was the most overpowering pitcher I've ever seen.

ryan and Ruth, on her parent's front porch in 1964.

Q

What was *your greatest thrill?*

People bring up the 5,000th strikeout, and the 300 wins, but those were a product of my longevity.

So it would have to be the no-hitters. The first one, with the Angels in 1973, at Kansas City, because I didn't think I was that

kind of pitcher – to hold a team hitless. The fourth one is a big memory because I tied Koufax.

But if I had to pick one moment, it would be the seventh no-hitter in 1991, in Arlington, against Toronto. I was 44 years old

and this was probably the best game I ever pitched. I had 16 strikeouts, 13 of them in the first 21 batters.

I got Roberto Alomar for the final out. His father, Sandy, had been my second baseman in my first two no-hitters.

The best part was, I did it in front of the Rangers fans, who had been so good to me.

Q

What does it mean for you to be elected to the *Hall of Fame?*

I'm humbled by it. When I went to the orientation (in early May), it really sank in.

When you walk into the Hall, and you look at the plaques and the displays there with all the great players, like Ty Cobb, Ruth, Gehrig, Cy Young, Walter Johnson, all of them, and they show you where your plaque is going to hang, you realize that you are going to be thought of on that level. You always held those people and what they accomplished in a special place. I wasn't one to compare myself to other players. During my career, when I was passing certain number plateaus, it was happening on a day-to-day basis in my life and I didn't give it much thought. I wasn't one to reflect on what was going on in my career.

I'm really never one to have studied the record books.

Then to walk to the no-hit display and see all the hats in there and see all the guys who have thrown no-hitters in the game, and see the separate display they have for my seven hats, was a neat feeling.

Q

Tell us about getting the call from the Hall of Fame. Why do you think you got such a *high percentage* of the vote?

A

We had all our kids home, our daughter Wendy, our sons Reid and Reese and their wives, and we weren't expecting a call, if it came, until one o'clock. We were getting ready to have lunch. It was about 12:30 and Reese was in the kitchen cooking fajitas.

I had just thought, "What if the call doesn't come?"

I had been reading and hearing that I was going to be voted in, but if you learn anything in baseball it's that nothing is certain.

Then the call came a half hour early, and there was a lot of cheering and laughing and hugging.

I don't know what to say about getting more than 98 percent, the second highest vote total in history. You think about all the great players, it doesn't seem possible. But when Governor Bush (the former co-owner of the Rangers) heard the news, he said he wanted to find the six writers who didn't vote for me.

Q

Do you have *any advice* for those running baseball today?

I think baseball needs for the pendulum to swing back to give the pitchers a break.

The home run derbies have been fun,

but the hitters have been dominant long enough. I think they need to raise the mound. Raising the strike zone didn't

accomplish anything. They can go back to calling the high strike, but there's probably not three pitchers, maybe four, in the big

leagues, who pitch upstairs. Very few pitch up and are effective. You affect so few that it's not going to have any impact.

You'd be better off widening the strike zone or calling the ball down (at the knees) more than the ball up. But the first thing

I would do is raise the mound. What it does is give you more leverage and change the plane of your pitches.

Physically, it's easier on you.

How do you want to be *remembered?*

A

As a guy who did everything he could to help his team win. As a guy who was going to prepare

and dedicate himself to do the best he could. I wanted fans to feel like they got their money's worth at the game.

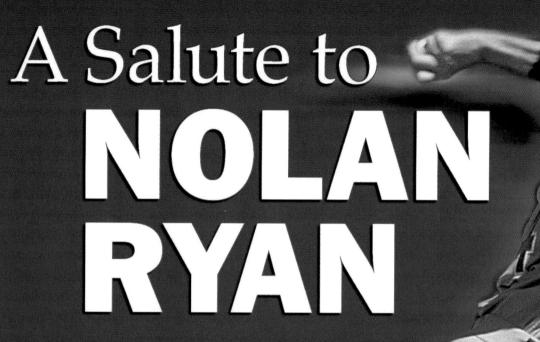

A Salute to
NOLAN
RYAN

New York Mets

California Angels

Houston Astros

Texas Rangers

Quotes and Memories

"If they had a higher league, he would be in it."

— *Hal McRae, former major leaguer*

"It's not something I'm ashamed about. I'm on a long, long list.
I'm in good company."

— *Rickey Henderson, on being the 5,000th strikeout victim*

"The first pitch I received from Nolan Ryan was up and in.
It was the most frightening pitch I've ever seen.
It just frightened me. I had some kind of phobia after that.
I just couldn't hit him."

— *Ron LeFlore, former major leaguer*

"Congratulations, Nolan Ryan. What an amazing accomplishment. Indeed, everybody that loves baseball pays tribute to you on this very special record-breaking occasion. Well done my friend, well done my noble friend."

— President George Bush, on the night Ryan recorded his 5,000th strikeout

"Strikeouts and no-hitters don't measure what he's meant to the game."

— Joe Garagiola, TV personality and former major leaguer

"He threw the ball harder than any pitcher I ever saw, including Sandy Koufax."

— Frank Robinson, fellow Hall of Famer

"He's the prototype power pitcher. He's the standard. He's superseded Carlton, Gibson and Seaver. You don't say, 'Does a guy throw as hard as Bob Gibson or Tom Seaver.' You say, 'Does he throw as hard as Nolan Ryan.' "

— Ted Simmons, former major leaguer

"Clemens is an outstanding pitcher, but there's not one pitcher who
could intimidate you like Nolan could.
He had that element of intimidation. You knew that
guy was not going to be an easy at-bat.
You had to have your stuff together to hit him."

— Toby Harrah, former major leaguer

"God gave Nolan the ability to throw a baseball faster than anybody else."

— Phil Garner, Astros teammate

"The best stuff of any pitcher I've ever seen. That was there from the start.
When the book closes on him, he will rank as the most
overpowering pitcher in history."

— Tom Seaver, fellow Hall of Famer

"You have to hand it to him. He's tough, as good as
he ever was ... a legend."

—*Paul Molitor, former Milwaukee Brewer (on the night Ryan earned his 300th victory)*

"He pumps gas. You either get him or he gets you."

— *Rickey Henderson*

"So many kids idolize him. So many kids were Nolan Ryan
when they played baseball in their backyards.
I was one of those kids."

— *Mike Greenwell, former major leaguer*

"The fact that he remained a power pitcher for so long is amazing.
With his stuff and longevity, if anyone broke my records,
I knew it would be him."

— *Sandy Koufax, fellow Hall of Famer*

"You could hear his ball hiss. It didn't sound like anyone else's.
Kind of like sssssst.
I used to tell young hitters, you don't need to run up there and hit it.
It will get there plenty quick,
and when it does, you better be ready to swing."

— *Hank Aaron, All-time home run king*

"I was a rookie and went up to the plate batting .090. He just stared at
me and gave me one of those get-in-there-and-stop-wasting-my-time looks.
I hit a long one that had a chance to be
a home run, but it curved foul. I was feeling pretty good about that,
and then I looked at him.
He was glaring at me, and I knew I was in trouble."

– *Len Matuszek, former major leaguer*

"That's all I have? I thought I had a lot more. I've always had great
success against fastballers, guys like Gooden and Clemens.
But Ryan's in a different category.
All the at-bats I've had against him have been bad."

— *Claudell Washington, who struck out 36 times against Ryan, most by any opponent*

"I met him in 1980 at the Astrodome. I was in high school
and I was in awe of him. He looked me in the eye and
made me feel real comfortable talking to him.
I really didn't do much of the talking. I mostly listened.
I remember thinking, 'Boy he really is a nice guy.' "

— *Roger Clemens, New York Yankee*

"There have been times when an umpire called a strike and
I told him the ball sounded low.
Really. You can see his fastball, but sometimes it's real hard.
Especially in twilight. He isn't like Gooden.
Dwight Gooden is tall and gets a lot of leverage and his ball rises.
Ryan comes from right behind his ear and the ball just gets there."

— *Steve Sax, former major leaguer*

"It helps if you don't tense up, because you might have to run for your life."

– *George Brett, fellow Class of '99 Hall of Famer*

"I spiked him on the heel when he was covering first (base)
on a ball that I had hit. I said I was sorry, but I guess he
never heard me because he never turned around. So I said to myself,
'I guess he's going to knock me down next time. And he did."

– Bert Campaneris, former major leaguer

"When a pitcher throws inside on a batter, causing the breeze
to whistle around his Adam's apple, baseball folks call it chin music.
The other day at Tucson, against Cleveland, Nolan Ryan played an
entire medley of his favorite tunes."

– Los Angeles Times, March 31, 1978

"Every time you looked up there was a better arm
coming out of the bullpen.
Tell me, what are they saving that Ryan for? That fastball of his,
you not only can't hit it, you can't even hear it."

— Boog Powell, former major leaguer

"You can evoke all the rhythm and flavor of baseball with one
freeze-frame of Ryan blowing a strike past a big hitter. Ryan in his windup,
his left knee nearly hiding his face, is one of the
imperishable portraits of sport."

— Mickey Herskowitz, The Houston Chronicle

"All athletes die young, except maybe Nolan Ryan."

– *Richard Reeves,* United Press Syndicate

"I tried to bunt off him and the next two pitches were right at my chest. I promised Nolan I wouldn't try to bunt off of him from then on. He made his point."

– *Mike Hargrove, former major leaguer*

"With Nolan, it was man against boys."

– *Alan Trammel, former major leaguer*

"I looked at Nolan Ryan and certain people just look like what they do ... he just looked like a pitcher."

– *Ernie Banks, fellow Hall of Famer*

"Nolan has one ingredient that just about every successful
pitcher has ... Nolan was pretty mean."

– *Frank Tanana, Angels teammate*

"Nolan and Sandy Koufax had the same mystique ... They were capable
of throwing a no-hitter each time they took the mound."

– *Frank Robinson, fellow Hall of Famer*

"Nolan was a guy you went to bed thinking about ..."

– *Dusty Baker, former major leaguer*

"When you step into the batters box against Nolan
the hair on the back of your neck sort of stands up. His presence
on the mound was about as intimidating as it got."

– *Wade Boggs, Tampa Bay Devil Ray*

"This is war ... I'm going to win ... I'm taking no prisoners."

– Frank Tanana on Ryan's attitude

"It was almost like playing with a legend when he was still playing."

– Art Howe, Astros teammate

"You give me a big game, I'll take Nolan Ryan,
I'll take Nolan Ryan all day ...
I'll take Nolan Ryan against the '27 Yankees."

– Pete Rose, All-time base hits king

"I had to catch him in the Rochester bullpen without lights. I chased as many as I caught. He can really throw smoke. When he gets the curve over for a strike, he will be another Sandy Koufax."

– Jackie Warner, Mets teammate

"All I can tell you is that the boy has a great arm. I had heard about it, but I had never seen it. Now that I have, I believe it."

– Gil Hodges, Mets manager, 1968-71

"He throws harder for one pitch than anyone I've ever seen."

– Bob Aspromonte, former major leaguer

"He's faster than instant coffee, wall-to-wall heat."

– Reggie Jackson, fellow Hall of Famer

"Ryan could throw the ball through a car wash without gettin' it wet."

– Durwood Merrill, AL umpire

"It's impossible not to like Nolan. Here is a guy who makes
so much money, yet his style of living and his concern for his family are
as genuine as with any person I've ever met. He is a man with class."

– *Terry Puhl, Astros teammate*

"He fit in from the moment he joined this club (Houston).
For all the pressure, all the strain he went through last year (as a
million-dollar athlete performing in his own backyard), he never
stopped being Nolan the team man, a guy we all rooted for and
cared about."

– *Joe Niekro, Astros teammate*

"He's fit in any place he went, any team, any business. He's his own
person. He goes about his business in a private way. At the park, he kids
with us and is simply one of the guys. But when he's got the ball and
takes the mound, you can see him change. He has that look about him
that says, 'Nobody is going to beat me.' He is such a gamer."

– *Joe Sambito, Astros teammate*

"Superman couldn't have hit him today once he started
getting his breaking ball over."

– *Tony Scott, Astros teammate*

"This is one tremendous feat. It shows consistency and longevity.
These are exactly the same kinds of ingredients that should automatically
put a player into the Hall of Fame."

– Al Oliver, former major leaguer (on Ryan breaking Walter Johnson's strikeout record)

"He stays in such great shape, he'll pitch as long as he wants to.
His accomplishments are a combination of everything - desire, ability,
durability and his competitiveness."

– Bob Lillis, Houston manager, 1982-85

"Nolan Ryan is not only as fine a performer, but as fine
a human being as any organization could have associated with it."

– Bobby Valentine, Rangers manager, 1985-92

"He's like the mailman, nothing keeps him from making his rounds.
I don't think the general public is aware of the effort he puts in."

– Tom House, Rangers pitching coach, 1985-92

"They should just open the doors of the Hall of Fame and put him in right now. He belongs there. He shouldn't have to wait five years."

– Merv Rettenmund, Oakland A's hitting instructor, 1989-90

"He's made the image of baseball No. 1 down here. He grew up in a football area, but now even football people think he's the greatest."

– Red Murff, scout who signed Ryan out of high school in 1965

"I'm about as plain as you can get. I know what I am, and I know who he is. But we were brought up alike. It doesn't matter how much money a person has. It's what he wants to be. I guess that's why my family has always liked him a lot. He is a genuine person. He's never forgotten his roots as a small-town person from Texas."

–Bill Gilbreth, long-time friend

"He could break all the records before he's through."

– Gil Hodges

"We had been at a cattle sale, and people had been bugging Nolan all day.
We go to this restaurant that's got good barbecue and great onion rings.
We're sitting there eating, and this table full of girls just starts looking at us.
Then one of 'em can't take it any longer.
She gets up and comes over to our table with a camera.
She says 'I'm sorry to bother you, but we're from New York and I've never
seen onion rings as big as those. Do you mind if I take a picture
of the onion rings?' They didn't know Nolan from Joe Blow. I told Nolan that
he should have held them up so when the pictures were
developed somebody would say, 'Hey, isn't that Nolan Ryan with the
onion rings?' It was great to see him get shot down by onion rings."

– Larry Phillips, long-time friend and neighbor

"It's unfair. When I was in the National League, we never swung at Ryan's
curveball. We knew it wasn't going to be over the plate. It's not fair for any
pitcher to have a curve like Ryan's, not if he has that fastball."

– Larry Hisle, former major leaguer

"He provides us with a legacy. For a franchise to have a tradition, it must have legends. Mickey Mantle, Joe DiMaggio and Babe Ruth are legends in New York. Nolan Ryan is a legend in Texas."

– George W. Bush, Texas governor

"The thing I'll get chills about wasn't the last out or any out in the ninth. The scene I'll remember is Nolan on the bench with his son rubbing his back and patting him on the leg, giving him a pep talk. No one else could bear to talk to him. That was a wonderful sight."

– Bobby Valentine (talking about the night of Ryan's sixth no-hitter)

"Every hitter likes fastballs, just like everybody likes ice cream. But you don't like it when someone's stuffing it into you by the gallon. That's how you feel when Ryan's throwing balls by you. You just hope to mix in a walk so you can have a good night and only go 0-for-3."

–Reggie Jackson, fellow Hall of Famer

"Has the best arm I've ever seen in my life. Could be a real power pitcher some day."

– Red Murff's scouting report on high school prospect Nolan Ryan

"It helps if the batter thinks you're a little crazy."

– Nolan Ryan

"When you talk velocity, Nolan threw the hardest. Nolan threw it down the strike zone harder than any human being I ever saw. In 1973 against the Red Sox, Nolan threw a pitch a little up and over my left shoulder. I reached up for it and Nolan's pitch tore a hole in the webbing of my glove and hit the backstop at Fenway Park."

– Jeff Torborg, Angels teammate

"Those were the best pitches I ever heard."

– Mickey Stanley, former major leaguer

"When my career is over, and I sit down at the gas station or wherever, and people ask me, 'What was one of your biggest moments?' I'll say, 'Facing Nolan Ryan.' "

– Glenn Wilson, former major leaguer

"I think when Nolan Ryan came to Texas he was a superstar and when he left he was a legend. He came to epitomize everything that was good in baseball, all the values that are enduring and why the people hold the game with so much affection. I can't think of anybody I'd rather have in the Hall of Fame."

– Tom Schieffer, Rangers president, 1991-present

"When he was on, forget it. You talk about guys being tough. When he was throwing the fastball, change and curve for strikes, it was a victory just getting the bat on the ball."

– Tony Gwynn, perennial NL batting champion

"The thing you marvel at is that he never varied his style. He didn't develop a knuckleball or go to being a curveball pitcher. He went to the end the way he pitched at the beginning."

– Tom Grieve, Texas Rangers general manager, 1984-94

"I was looking for a fastball, Ryan threw a curve and
I got vapor-locked."

– Brad Mills, former major leaguer (Ryan's 3,509th strikeout, pushing him past Walter Johnson's all-time strikeout record)

"Nolan knows he has perfect mechanics. It makes no difference
that he doesn't understand the mechanics. He lucked into throwing the ball
right. It came naturally to him. If he had been taught,
he probably wouldn't do it right."

– Dr. Mike Marshall, former major leaguer

"Ryan's the best. He's the only guy in baseball today who, every time
he takes the mound, he's capable of a no-hitter. I get the damnedest kick out
of people who say he shouldn't be in the Hall of Fame. If he's not in the
Hall of Fame, there shouldn't be a Hall of Fame.
That's me talking, the all-time hit leader who faced him 15 years.
He ought to have his own building in Cooperstown."

– Pete Rose, all-time base hit king

"He's spectacular. With someone like Ryan there is always the possibility of a strikeout record or a no-hitter."

– Herb Score, Cleveland Indians broadcaster and former major leaguer

"He's like Joe DiMaggio. You respond to him. There's a sense of majesty."

– Al Rosen, former major leaguer and baseball executive

"I was one of the lucky ones to be present at County Stadium in Milwaukee when Nolan Ryan won his 300th game. It was a fitting tribute to one of the few pitchers who seemed to improve with age. He was a true marvel, his fastball as unhittable at the end of his career as it was at the beginning. I feel privileged to have witnessed this remarkable athlete throughout his long and historic career."

– Allan "Bud" Selig, Major League Baseball Commissioner

"Nolan Ryan is the Jimmy Stewart of professional athletes. Both were all-time greats in their chosen fields and enjoyed careers that extended well into their later years. And, of course, each had 'a wonderful life.'"

– Matt Merola, agent for over 28 years

"Who says there are no heroes anymore? I believe in true American heroes and Nolan Ryan is one such man.
'Modesty,' 'Determination,' 'Class'– these all add up to Nolan Ryan, a great ball player, a great man, a hero!"

– President George Bush

"My ability to throw was a gift.
A God-given gift."

– Nolan Ryan

"This is indeed a special day and I am privileged to be here."

"I truly do believe that I was blessed by a lot of people whose paths crossed mine as I went down the road of my career."

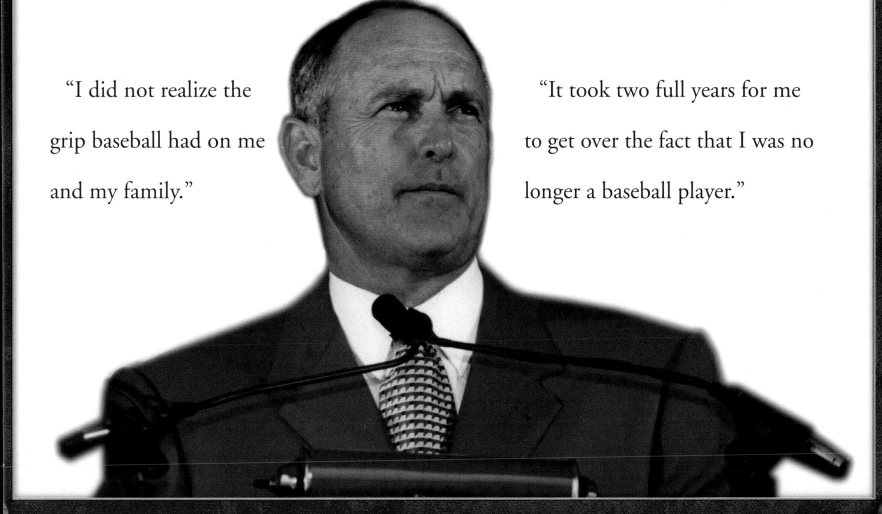

"I did not realize the grip baseball had on me and my family."

"It took two full years for me to get over the fact that I was no longer a baseball player."

"I like to refer to my years with the Angels as the foundation of my career."

"The years in Houston ... gave us the opportunity to live in Texas ..."

"I've never enjoyed an organization more than the Texas Rangers."

"I feel very fortunate to have played for the four organizations I did ... I was blessed by the fans ... and the support that they gave me ... and that's what makes this a great game ... I may be gone, but I won't forget you. I appreciate all those times that you supported me and my family over the 27 years that I played."

Nolan Ryan

Welcome to the Hall of Fame, Nolan Ryan.

New York Mets
1966-71

California Angels
1972-79

Houston Astros
1980-88

Texas Rangers
1989-93